Screenplay Form
and Structure

On-Demand Publishing, LLC

Tumwater, WA 98051

First Edition

ISBN 978-1477644782

PREFACE

Zoetrope is a great place for someone learning to really get raw critique and have people pick their stuff apart, while learning methods they may not have been familiar with. The best thing for someone new to do is get invited into the private office of a writer whose work they may admire and share ideas.

-- Wes Laurie, writer/producer

I joined Zoetrope in 2003. At the time I was a modestly notorious, if not quite famous expat writer and filmmaker living in rural Costa Rica. My last link to Los Angeles and London was a crappy 56K modem attached to one of the world's worst landlines.

Before pluerisy and a bout of paranoia forced me to quit a year later, I reviewed 23 Zoetrope scripts and hosted a fairly busy private office called The A-List. Those were really the salad days, when you could put development and production deals together on Zoetrope. An 'A-List' pal in New York pitched Harvey Weinstein for me. Later, I went to bat for Lola Teigland, an amazingly talented screenwriter and member of the A-List office. Rob Anderson produced a short. Wendy Henson had a development deal. There was shock and pain when I shut the A-List door and disappeared.

Flash forward to 2010. With a brainy young wife and a cute young daughter who sings and tells jokes – jeez, how lucky can a guy get? -- I found myself unable to process the emotional strain of creative writing and gave up, intellectually empty and beaten, after trooping to five continents in five years. We were snuggled warm and safe in a serene Colorado snowdrift. I had plenty of free time and little to do except an 800-word weekly column for a magazine in Abu Dhabi.

So, I rejoined Zoetrope. Much had changed. I spent several weeks searching the Screenplay, Short Scripts and Short Story boards and found lots of warm-hearted human beings who knew how to write.

One by one, I invited them to gather at a new private office called 'The B-List.' The front door had a fresh welcome mat: "Generally supportive of young writers and filmmakers. Questions answered." – and a stern sticky note: *Will read comedy, action-adventure, westerns. No horror.*

What you're about to read is a treasury of our conversations and real-world practical knowledge of screenwriting, story development and marketing your work. 'The B-List' was blessed by industry veterans and working pros who responded magnificently to questions by talented newcomers.

Somewhere along the line, I invented a butler named Col. Mustard to tend bar, and more often than not his fictional antics kept the party going late at night, when all decent people had their doors and windows bolted against such deplorable tomfoolery.

Special thanks to Jim Kalergis for permission to include his fabulous posts on audience bonding, rewrites, and pro script analysis.

Alan von Altendorf

CONTRIBUTORS

Jim Kalergis

Brian A Young

Dave Pauwels

Sally Lewis

RLB Hartmann

Heather McLoud

David Shelley

Tom Deaver

Tony Contreras

Ken Kleeman

Jonas Knutsson

Erik Svehaug

John Prohaska

Stephan A. Foley

Derek Finney

Margaret Langendorf

Bill Sherwood

Naomi James

Barry S. Cowan

Rob Williamson

Lucy Sogoian

Frank J. Meuller III

Julie Ann Young

Barry Friesen

Chris Keaton

Gregor Mac

John Corral

Gerry Byron

Gareth Penner

Marty Zeigler

Jay Schay

Writing

as a career and a
workplace experience

The joy, thrill, and pain of writing

ALAN ~

Since we have a few moments to ourselves, no urgent business pending, let's talk about writing as a career and a workplace experience. I wrote full-time temporary, as opposed to part-time or permanent. Which means: when I started a project, I worked at it daily and continuously until it was finished.

There were exceptions of course. I had to quit *The Good Walk Alone* after 16 weeks, because I went on strike. But the exception wasn't very exceptional. I never wrote another word on that project. It's very difficult for me to pick up a half-finished story and rekindle the sense of momentum it once had. Storytelling is an adventure, very similar to a romance. Break the spell of love-making and it ends badly and bitterly. I was never businesslike or workmanlike. I was consumed, enthralled, incapable of much else in life when working on a story.

Revisions are another matter entirely. It's good to revisit a completed work a year or two later. Fresh eyes see new opportunities. Comments made by literary agents and friendly readers finally sink in. Problems get fixed.

Assignments were more, not less consuming.

A WRITER'S TEMPLE (G21 Magazine, Feb. 2000) -- It didn't take long. Folks are upset because fate handed me a mansion on the Pacific, no job, no bills, no household chores (cocktail parties and fan mail optional). Temporarily rich, I'm learning how to push an intercom button and order breakfast when I feel like it in the morning. Queenie bought a young chestnut stallion, hand picked by the gardener's brother. A fine horse indeed, according to its trainer -- and heartily concurred by our housekeeper, the relief housekeeper, the downstairs maid, and a leatherfaced blacksmith.

But if I'm going to be envied for anything, I'd rather be scolded for having a writer's temple. If you don't have one, be assured it is the goal of all human industry -- farms, oil wells, semi-conductor factories, etc. Paradoxically, I did very little to achieve possession of a writer's temple. You can set one up for about 30 cents, and it's completely portable. I've carried this particular temple around the planet with me for the better part of two decades. It fits with any decor (although a bare room is best). Here are the specs:

- desk
- chair
- computer
- printer
- lamp
- bed

So what makes it a temple? -- Chrissie Hynde tonight, Led Zeppelin tomorrow, and a minimum of contact with the outside world, including my wife. We get together between bouts of writing that run for a day or two, before I overheat and need hospitalization. My recurring mental exhaustion doesn't play well in Queenie's boudoir, so I limit my time in the temple to six or seven hours a day, and I learned to take a lot of leisurely breaks. Having houseguests has been helpful (provided that they leave after a few days). But temple life doesn't end simply because I take time off. Indeed, time away must end in my return. I always return to writing, whether I want to or not.

That's why my temple is a masterpiece of efficiency. Left to right on the desk top are: carton of Marlboro, telephone, intercom, legal pad, stack of CDs, ashtray, small pile of notes, coffee cup, mouse pad, and a big empty area to park stuff in transit.

People ask me to read things. They sit in the Transit Area for a month or two and ultimately get shoved in a drawer. In the event that I have to relocate my writing temple, the desk drawers are emptied, and I say a little ceremonial "Hmm" over a black plastic trash bag, to honor the forgotten. These paper orphans are omelet parts, in the sense that they sacrifice their thin, rectangular lives, so that my temple is not defiled by accounting statements, story outlines, or vital correspondence. I follow an exacting rule, adapted from the One Minute Manager: handle everything only once, and put all of it immediately in a thick, neat pile that deters further involvement.

I cannot write any other way. The temple computer is always on, and my screen has no games, no cutesy icons, no ICQ flower. Bookmarks are few: just G21 and two other publication venues, and an archive of my defunct website. This last item shows how hard it is to achieve defunctnitude on the web. I cancelled my London mirror account more than a year ago, and repeatedly begged them by email to delete the subdomain. All I achieved was to lock myself out of their firewall, and the site is still live, proving that this author does not comprehend the Internet.

It's highly debatable that I understand anything at all, since story outlines are useless to me. I pen them in good faith. But however daring and clever, an outline only controls one character, usually less than a week or two -- which is enough to belt out the first chapter. From there, the story takes off on its own, surprising me with situations and personalities over which I have no direct control. The temple has its own agenda, it's own mad logic of dramatic necessity. All I do is show up to write about it.

Therefore, a temple. Sometimes it's frightening and lonely and empty. I feel like shit and walk away. The story follows me to the kitchen, to the driveway, to a sunset or the night sky. I whistle for the dogs and pretend that I'm a normal person --- that, no matter what, I'm just as fit as the next fellow to have a private life, I can eat a meal or chat with houseguests. Writers tell themselves lies like that, to avoid the truth of the temple. Quality doesn't matter much, nor hope. The essence of the issue is a blank page and the willingness to go naked in public. As far as I know, Victor Hugo already beat me hands down. What remains is a precious window of courage, to let it happen and let it be.

JIM ~

> *"Quality doesn't matter much, nor hope. The essence of the issue is a blank page and the willingness to go naked in public. As far as I know, Victor Hugo already beat me hands down. What remains is a precious window of courage, to let it happen and let it be."*

Nice, Alan. Maybe I'm not as alone as I thought.

I've always figured those who boast about how much fun writing is aren't doing it right. (Only half kidding here.)

My very best writing is born of emotional and even physical pain, often when I'm under the enormous pressure of a seemingly hopeless deadline.

And yes, the process might take me to a place I've been avoiding, yet in the end, I'm a better person for the experience.

BRIAN ~

Great post. Perfect timing as I sit down to re-write.

FRANK ~

Writing is painful, Alan? Since when, and to whom? Explain, please.

BILL ~

It is to me, always. It's like giving birth. And all the time trying to cope with the corrosive doubt 'Is this good enough?' and the growing feeling of loneliness. Not everyone feels this way, but I'm not unique by any means. But, hey, what a buzz when something is eventually finished and I feel that it is the best I can do.

FRANK ~

Why do you willingly do anything that brings you pain?

BILL ~

Why do you willingly do anything that brings you pain?

If women adopted that attitude, none of us would have been born.

ALAN ~

Ernest Hemingway, suicide. Scott Fitzgerald, alcoholic dead at age 44. Herman Melville, pauper. O Henry, convict and wastrel. Sylvia Plath, suicide. Virginia Woolf, suicide. Speaking for myself, the pressure of excellence is so severe as a novelist that I have many times struggled with anger, insanely violent and suicidal impulses. A few weeks ago I recognised the deadly symptoms and put aside my current project *Dreamland*. That's why I came to Zoetrope. I do not need to prove anything to myself or anyone else at this stage of life by self-destruction for art.

And now I will tell a little story.

About a hundred years ago when digital referred exclusively to fingers and radio tubes got hot, I was at my desk in another fellow's office, slowly considering the nicest possible way to ghostwrite a speech. The chairman of a grocery chain had to explain why his empire was underperforming by a factor of thirty and that everything would be better next quarter, when the phone rang. Back in those days, telephones had bells and curlicue cords that ended in a handset heavy enough to kill an intruder if he happened to intrude within three or four feet of the desk.

My girlfriend was crying, in a desperate state, convinced she was having a heart attack. I sighed, turned off the switch on my noisy Selectric II, and inquired with suitable patience and sympathy whatever was wrong, dear? "I can't breathe," she gasped. "My chest is pounding. I've been trying to write a script and I can't do anything without getting confused and I keep making mistakes and wasting paper and I can't do this! Do you think I'm having a heart attack?"

"No, darling," I affirmed. "You're having an art attack."

"Oh, no!" she wailed, as if that was worse. "What's an art attack?"

I thereupon improvised the following nonsense, because I wanted this interruption ended as quickly as possible. I'm capable of many heroisms, but ghostwriting a pack of lies for a grocery store magnate is not the sort of thing I can do in fits and spurts. Connected, logical-sounding horsefeathers are a delicate chore. "Okay, let me see if I understand the situation. You type a few words or a couple lines, and then it all looks like garbage, right?"

"Yes!" she bawled. "I'm writing garbage! I can't even spell correctly!"

"Look honey, you need to understand what Art is. Art is leaning over your shoulder, watching everything you do. You're self-conscious and upset and hyperventilating because Art keeps telling you that you're writing garbage, right?"

"Uh... yeah, I guess so, metaphorically or something."

"Okay. Pay attention. This is important. Art is a garbage collector. He's a big fat guy wearing a smelly old T-shirt that has holes in it, he's smoking the stub of a cigar, and he has no aesthetic judgment or sympathy. He's there bugging you and making you miserable be-cause he's thinks you're a writer and that all writers write garbage. All he wants is the garbage. Put a fresh piece of paper in the machine, type a bunch of garbage, gibberish, anything, then rip it out, ball it up and throw it over your shoulder to Art. He'll have some garbage and he'll go away and leave you alone, so you can relax and write."

She did as I asked, somewhat skeptically, typed some awful crap with abundant misspellings, ripped it from her typewriter, balled it up and tossed it over her shoulder. Art the Garbage Collector was duly assuaged and left the apartment. She was very appreciative and had a nice new comedy script for me to giggle at over dinner that evening.

Cut to Hollywood a dozen years later. My girlfriend was given an important introduction to one of Tinsel Town's oldest, most respected and successful television distributors, the late Arthur Greenfield. She came back from Greenfield's Wilshire Boulevard office looking like a dazed survivor. I asked how it went?

"You're not going to believe this," she said solemnly. "The secretary was at lunch and his office door was open. He said: *'Come on in, sweetie! I been expectin ya.'* I walked into his office. He had enormous floor-to-ceiling bookshelves on both walls, like a library, thousands of reels of videotape masters: Lassie, My Three Sons, the old Max Fleischer Popeye series, What's My Line, Charlie's Angels, almost every off-network series I've ever heard of. Art Greenfield was sitting behind a big desk, smoking a cigar. He had a T-shirt with holes in it. He waved his hand at the shelves and said -- you're not gonna believe this, Wolf -- he said: *'See all this? Garbage! All garbage!'*

"I met Art," she whispered with awe. "You were right. He's a garbage collector." True story I swear.

BILL ~

True or not - and I believe you - it's an excellent one. Thanks.

JIM ~

Writing truly great characters requires that the writer squarely face up to and confront the human condition in all its splendor, glory, pain, and horror. That may very well be a painful experience. In

8

regione caecorum rex est luscus. ("In the land of the blind, the one-eyed man is king.") Desiderius Erasmus

ALAN ~

I didn't want to write Danny, but there wasn't much choice in the matter. I had to show evil as a tangible, credible threat -- the product of a permissive, stupefied gentry of dumbbells. Faced with the duty of writing Danny, I asked a number of colleagues for advice: What is evil? John Young challenged me to define it myself. "You'll have to look inside," he concluded.

I looked and found Danny, who frightened and revulsed me. That's why I say an author is stripped naked, and it takes courage to write fiction, as much courage as you dare.

[preface, MARS SHALL THUNDER]

Reading Pro Scripts

SALLY ~

I need, and want, to read more scripts. I've been going through DailyScript.com and trying to read a script a day. (I'll fall short, without a doubt, but it's a goal worth aiming for.)

One of the limitations is I'd like to see the film version before I read the script, where possible.

Ideally, I'd like to work my way, viewing and reading, through the WGA 's 101 Greatest Screenplays of All Time list.

If anyone else has suggestions of scripts that stand out and are worth reading as scripts, I welcome your recommendations.

Is anyone interested in reading scripts together and comparing notes?

Edited to add:

I'm just as interested in reading non-English scripts -- either scripts in French, which I can read, or international scripts in translation. Does anyone have suggestions for similar lists from other countries, or for sources of international screenplays?

BRIAN ~

Have you checked out gointothestory.com?

He has lists and links to must read scripts in many genres and why they are all a "must read." It's a great blog and he posts regularly.

About authorship

ALAN ~

Some thoughts about writing.

I am extremely supportive of new work, with extra credit for creativity and fulsome praise for storytelling skill of any kind. It gives me great pleasure to read your hard-won literature and your finely crafted scripts. I know the sort of dedication it takes to do good work. I wish I had the power to publish and produce everything, which is impossible. My contacts are as stale as dry cheese. My pockets are nearly as empty as yours. Occasionally (okay, rarely) I can help a little. It wasn't always so.

At the height of my career arc, it was easy to let the creative power of others' high-voltage lightning strike me on the noggin and to get things done. Nowadays, I need an afternoon nap. A retired indie director is about as useful as a busted doorstop. The most I seem to do fairly well is to offer encouragement and spread an atmosphere of welcome and good cheer.

Yet it matters that someone should honestly see merit in your best work, and it's important to be reasonably fair -- offering greatest enthusiasm for work that succeeds in touching a distant, previously unexplored star.

It's damned difficult being original. So, I'm an easy friend, ready to acknowledge achievement of many styles and progress in the general direction of originality. This is not an interesting discussion as yet. I'll get to the point as quickly as possible.

As you can perhaps imagine I, too, aimed at originality and adroit use of time, imagery and characterization. From time to time, many years ago, reasonably bright people thought I was a reasonably good author and playwright. From time to time I was published and produced and praised. That wasn't the problem.

The problem was Roger Daltry.

Since I listen to classic rock on the radio, I hear Daltry often, and it still makes me mad, every damn time. How can someone in the swim of creative life be such a dope?

I wrote a pretty wonderful script called THE GUITAR PLAYER FROM THE BLACK LAGOON. I had enough clout to put a deal together, provided we had a star attached. A London exec who was doing music clearance on another project for me read GUITAR PLAYER and laughed his head off.

He said he'd get it to Daltry who was another of his many clients. Perfect. Great casting. And Daltry was looking for a movie.

Word came back: *"He said he didn't understand it."*

Gentle folk, there is no arguing with blockheads, no matter how good your work is, nor how perfect it would be for everybody concerned. This applies to publishers, agents, producers, stars, and audiences. Originality is box office poison 99 times out of 100.

I was an energetic young spirit forged by derring-do and achieved much as a journeyman writer/director. None of my career wins were remotely original. I did what producers and audiences wanted -- which was crap most of the time.

It gave me contacts and credentials to kick open doors and pitch signature work I cared about. The reaction was polite indifference.

When I became more adamant about original work and had the power to make it happen, it was deemed "old fashioned and roman- tic" -- the mark of death in a trendy world.

So, the bottom line is yes.

Write what moves you, win lose or draw. Fight for it.

BILL ~

Gentle folk, there is no arguing with blockheads...

Hidden behind these seemingly simple words is a true pearl of wisdom, learned from bitter experience -- and it applies in ANY walk of life.

MARGARET ~

Around here, we say, "you can't fix stupid." So true.

HEATHER ~

More or less succinctly put. I've had many well-meaning friends say, "You write beautifully but why don't you make some money by churning out popular novels like romances or thrillers?" Okay. Assuming I could just pick up my pen and write something trite everyone wanted to read? I don't want to! So, yes. I shall continue following the contorted path lit only by a muse with a flickering lantern. Half the challenge is losing her, pressing my nose to the ground, and sniffing out her trail again. Mixed metaphors and all.

The Panic-Stricken Writer

NAOMI ~

I used to write just because I wanted to -- because I had stories to tell, even if I was just telling them to myself -- because it's fun and rewarding in itself. Sure, it was something of a compulsion, but it's not like I've got any psychological demons. It's just who I am. I am a writer. And yeah I drink too much, and I don't have a proper job. These are not things I aspire, or ever aspired, to. It's just the way they worked out. They're sources of guilt. Free-spirited? Hell, no.

Since my first option everything feels different. There's pressure now. I have to meet the demands of others. I have to make the most of this opportunity. I have to get some scripts polished to approach agents with, while I can still say I have a script under option.

I keep asking myself, am I really any good at this? Are my stories really good enough? Do I really have anything unique to offer? Is this really what I even want for my future? I never had to think about that before. Who the hell am I, anyway?

I'm writing for different reasons now. I'm writing in a state of panic, desperate to make this thing pay off. Is it good enough? Is it good enough? Will it ever be? And always worrying that maybe I should be trying harder to make some more money now, but knowing if I got a full-time job again, if I could even find one, I'd be more miserable and I'd be less able to pursue the part-time positive things that I enjoy but bring in a pittance. Wondering if the generations upon generations of 'kept' women before me felt as guilty as I feel (most of them had kids to look after, I guess). Looking for purpose, with all my eggs in one rickety basket. Sorry. Just venting.

I've just come off a few days of TV 'extra' work -- a Visa commercial and a TV drama/doc about the riots in London. Exhausting stuff but good fun -- I got to dress up in police riot gear and everything!

14

Sadly not well paid though.

I started 'extra-ing' not because I want to be on camera but so I could get on a film set and see what goes on -- see what it takes to film a scene and so on. It's been a great education so far.

DAVID ~

Naomi, this is raw and very helpful. Thank you for sharing.

I am so fixated on getting to a certain point with my own work and it is getting there, or at least seems to be, but then I am aware of what is to come potentially and what that may look like, and yet emotionally, I had not considered elements of how some of that may feel and how it would be to navigate and you articulated it beautifully.

I watched a design show recently and the designer said if he had known what it took to run a design company when he started he never would have started. I think the process of developing as a writer is clearly different from the process of the actual professional work as one faces the different projects and nuances involved in changing scripts in this way or that or working with actors and directors at times to convey this or that, or rewrite something for their needs/wants.

There are tiers to develop and tears to be shed from the sounds of it. I think a lot of us figure the angst will end in some ways and maybe some of it will, or can, but there is new angst, or at least new things one can be angsty about.

I personally appreciate your 'venting' as it is a reality check in some ways. Sobering.

In my own work I am having some really nice growth and refinement occurring and have opened up to a couple close friends about a project in development and have gotten some good feedback which has been helpful in further sorting out the details. I continue to feel like my interest in TV writing is an elephant that is almost impossible to eat, but I keep putting one foot in front of the other. It feels like a thousand (or perhaps five thousand?) piece puzzle sometimes that I am struggling to assemble.

ROB ~

Nothing like being on a set. I did a lot of extra and Driver's work, beside an occasional speaking role. Crew Services turned me on. You'd get the breakfast burritos and a fine cuppa in the a.m. and some kinda fancy lunch and dinner later on. They'd usually have a "Dr. Ivers" (Drivers) trailer with bunks, refer, table, chairs, etc we'd get to use, but we just needed a place to burn one and crash. The hours can be long, as you know.

You were questioning whether yer good enuf ???

There's no doubt about that. I read your script; a couple versions. When you finished it the first time it was good enuf. It garnered interest to attract a director, etc. Nothing's changed. These are just hoops to jump through.

ALAN ~

Haven't read the other responses yet.

Your questions:

am I really any good at this? **Yes.**

Are my stories really good enough? **Yes.**

Do I really have anything unique to offer? **Yes.**

Is this really what I even want for my future? **Karma.**

Nobody really wants to be who they are, ma'am.

"I am painfully aware of apparent individuality and diversity, six billion unique lifestyles and hairstyles and nicknames. That's not the problem. The problem is that no one truly wishes to be who they are. I had hoped for a life like David Lean or Stanley Kubrick. In a pinch, I would have settled for Fred Zinneman. What I got instead was Wolf DeVoon -- an isolated beatnik with a second-class brain, whose idea of a good time is a newspaper and a cup of coffee at Denny's."

Creative power

ALAN ~

I have a difficult time with mobility in the morning, stiff as a board, takes a while to get up the stairs. Quite an ordeal putting on pants. I've been retired almost a year. Once in a while I can muster a few words of fact or opinion, but damn few, without much fire. In respect of my loss and a clear recollection of how it used to be, I'll mention the character of creative power in honor of yours. At heart, I'm still a bomb thrower, eager to energize others to throw a thousand more.

Curiosity

All stories begin and end with What If?

Passion

Writing burns brightly late at night, launches the new day like a bloodthirsty buccaneer, and makes lunch an optional nuisance postponed forgotten.

Intolerance

The music must be right, complete solitude, bills shoved underfoot or thrown in the trash. If there's a job, it's a writing job or lonely work with inherent drama. No writing gets done in a cubicle or a church.

Vanity

Creative license is everything. It's self-issued, selfish and personal, renewed minute by minute until your destiny is an ironclad done deal, all rights all media in perpetuity. Some people describe the hell of compulsion, forced to write or paint an unseen landscape. Fine. Be a victim of destiny. It's still a golden goose that no one wins in a cheery grade school lottery. The key is a root driven deep in the clay of one's soul to proclaim: "This is Me and Mine."

ROB ~

By God, where's the Colonel? We need to toast your message, Al.

ALAN ~

He said something about redecorating today...

JIM ~

George Bernard Shaw got it right when he said: "Youth is wasted on the young."

ALAN ~

Er ... very nice, Mustard. Very interesting and well shot, old boy!

May I have the revolver?

Please.

Bloody butler reminds me of something P.G. Wodehouse said:
"Just when a chap is feeling particularly braced with things in general, Fate sneaks up behind him with a bit of lead piping."

ROB ~

That's a hoot and so true. I needed to laugh...

HEATHER ~

Sitting here this evening with time blocked out for writing. Afraid to open the novel – even though I promised myself (threatened myself)

I would work on it the minute I finished the latest short story. Poking around your office instead of writing, I found this and feel pretty good now about not opening the novel. I believe I'll just open a blank page and write bits of the novel that appeal to me and worry about linearity and such later. Thanks.

LUCY ~

I find that is the best way to write anything, whether imaginative writing or non-fiction prose: create first, then "write" during the revision process, making it linear, details, exciting, scary, funny, or whatever is needed to make it good.

I guess since all writing begins with an idea, possibly some pre-writing notes and a blank page/screen where the writer takes nothing and creates something, all first drafts, no matter what type you are doing, are creative -- even the drab, narcoleptic stuff such as legal briefs, physics textbooks, how to work your new iPad and the like. It's the revision where the real writing (and for imaginative stuff, especially, the work), comes in. So I guess with this rather mad logic, the first draft should be called a "creation draft" and the 'second draft' is actually the first draft.

This has made me think of the differences between North America and Europe in Ground floor - 1st Floor - 2nd Floor delineations. Time to hide the tequilla!

HEATHER ~

You're right, of course. But that's a new way for me to look at it. Probably a lot of my perennial writer's block comes from my deleterious habit of writing chronologically. Instead of writing what I know will happen I try to write what happens NEXT! Thanks for the insight.

20

ALAN ~

Heather, I'm a fan. And you've given me a glimpse of this project which I appreciate very sincerely. No reason to write in strict continuity if there's a scene (a chapter) that's screaming to write itself.

About a year ago, I posted an explanation of Scene Cards that are used in organizing a movie screenplay. I mention it now because scenes (chapters) are the stuff of storytelling.

My mentor, Alejandro Rey, encouraged me to write the scenes of a story in any order or "out of order" to be organized later:

Before you write, you must think of scenes. The scenes. Here, tell me each scene you have planned. On the card I only write the characters' names, the place, and the action — in one word. What is the next? — And the next? — Now, look, is it better that he fights, he goes away, he feels ashamed, he has hope? Or maybe that he has hope, he fights, and he feels ashamed? By moving the cards you can try many, many ideas — then you write.

You have a great start. You need a great finish. What happens in between is important, of course, but it can be huge, complex, bitter, mysterious, tense -- really anything. A novel takes time to wrestle into final form. The nice thing about computers is that you can jot notes, leave big blank spaces to revisit later, work backwards from a known ending, etc.

I'm 100% supportive. I don't say that often. Write whatever sparks your energy and creative power.

HEATHER ~

I'm touched. And encouraged. And I have a ready supply of 3x5 cards which now have a use. I believe I'll sign off and give myself permission to imagine scenes – out of order even. Again, thanks for the support and encouragement.

Who reads a screenplay?

ALAN ~

Following up on Rob's 'Show and Tell' thread, and without making a distinction between screenplay and old style shooting script, here are some of the people who will read your submission with production in mind:

Story Department

First a reader, then a mid-level exec, who know what the producer is looking for in terms of story, budget, and marketing. They read a lot of scripts (mostly agented or solicited) and clean, easy to read screenplay format is appreciated.

Producer, Star, and Funding Counterparties

The producer has to read it, if he's going to pitch this project. No one makes movies without a distribution deal, TV presale, or star attached. Clean, easy to read screenplay format again. Numbered pages. Flashbacks and dream sequences must be clearly marked and make sense.

Production Manager

In order to pitch a project and make a production deal, someone has to do a budget breakdown. How many scenes? where? How many principal cast, day players, bits and extras? Wardrobe? Props? Picture cars, animals? Stunts? Special effects or computer work? How big a crew and how many crew days? Second unit? Allow for camera rentals, transportation, catering, post, insurance, blah blah blah.

Production Design, Art Department, Props

Very early in the planning stages, sometimes before there is a production deal or star attached, a production designer will be called in to sketch set design and some key scenes, especially for sci-fi and period pictures.

Director and Casting Director

Nobody makes a movie without lining up a director, who will probably want to read the screenplay. Casting is a big job. The script has to be read by actors, agents, managers, actor spouses, hair-dressers, astrologers, etc.

Assuming the project gets packaged and funded...

Department Heads

Dir of Photography
Choreographer
Stunt Coordinator
Location Scout
Set Designer
Wardrobe
Prop Master
Composer
Unit Manager

ROB ~

Well, by God, there it is, and the point is, your script has to be understood and theoretically imagined by most if not all.

Audience
and Protagonist
Bonding

Part One

The Audience/Protag Connection

JIM ~

Here's part 1 of the promised treatise.

For whatever reason, there's not a lot written on this subject. Yet it's hugely important that aspiring screenwriters understand what the "connection factor" is and how to achieve it.

I've found that the following football game analogy is the quickest way to get across the importance of the connection factor.

PRO FOOTBALL GAME NUMBER ONE

You have no connection to either team or their respective quarterbacks.

No connection = No interest = Not sucked in.

Worry-over-the-outcome factor: You're not engaged at all, 1 on a scale of 1 to 10.

Post-game emotional reaction, regardless of who wins = Big yawn.

PRO FOOTBALL GAME NUMBER TWO

You've followed this quarterback over the years. He's a noble soul and a good man. His father died last week. There was some question if he would start, but in the end he decided to play because his dad would have wanted it that way. He's dedicating the game to his dad.

You have a fairly good connection to this quarterback and his team.

Good connection = Good interest = Sucked in.

Worry-over-the-outcome factor: You're well-engaged, 5 on a scale of 1 to 10.

Post game emotional reaction after narrow win = A little adrenalin, and a big YES!

PRO FOOTBALL GAME NUMBER THREE

The quarterback is your son. The regular quarterback and his backup are both out with injuries. This is your kid's first start as a pro in a regular season game. The press is all over your boy, and his team is a twenty-one point underdog against last year's super bowl winners.

You have a super-strong connection to this quarterback and his team.

Super-strong connection = Super-strong interest = Major suck job! (if you'll pardon the expression.)

Worry-over-the-outcome factor -- You're fully engaged, 10 on a scale of 1 to 10.

Post game emotional reaction after the narrow win or even a good effort = A major adrenalin rush and perhaps even a spontaneous little dance.

Get the idea?

If you take a look over your movie-going history, you'll no doubt be able to recall a few films with exceptionally high connection factors. Recalling those with very low connection factors is more difficult, for the obvious reason.

In Part Two, we'll take a look at techniques for creating a strong audience/protag connection.

ROB ~

Jim... There's hardly a writer I enjoy more, hearing how to write screenplays, primarily because what you say makes sense.

I just got off work so am going to save this for the morn and a Mocha.

Thanks!

BILL ~

First, let me say thank you for this and how I look forward to reading Part 2.

Second, you are correct when you say that this is a hugely important subject but that not a great deal is written about it. In fact I've seen it mentioned only in a couple of books -- one of which was an academic work by a psychologist -- but neither explained how one can establish this 'connection' with the audience.

Third, this is a subject which should definitely be put into Alan's forthcoming book as it is one of the most important, if not THE most important aspect of screenwriting, in my opinion.

Yours aye,

Bill

JIM ~

You're welcome, Bill. I'll try and get part 2 posted in the next day or two.

It is rather strange how this aspect of storytelling seems to go unnoticed. Perhaps it's one of those things that's obvious only after it's pointed out.

I'm fine on having that post and the one that will follow in the book as long as you omit the vowels I, E, and sometimes Y. But seriously, in my forthcoming book *Screenwriting for Smart People* this subject will be greatly expanded upon, and this taste from my book in the B-List book could only help by generating interest in my work.

ALAN ~

> *omit the vowels I, E, and sometimes Y*

Deal.

Jim's analogy of the football games made me think of THE HUNGER GAMES, where the audience was bonded in their millions by the YA books promoted in elementary and middle schools nationwide. Hollywood has a long history of piggybacking on bestsellers, musical theater, straight plays, the Bible, etc.

JULIE ANN ~

I wonder if writers have a hard time connecting with people because they are anti-social. My first love was acting. I started writing once I realized I could portray all the characters on the page. The need to steal the show comes natural to me, but in order to accomplish that I have to be able to manipulate my audience. In order to manipulate humans you have to be able to emotionally connect with them. As many of you know, I can make a normal, rational human being morph him/her into a raging manic in a matter of seconds. When I work as a salesperson I utilize this talent in the opposite direction because I have to make my clients like me. Writers need to not only manipulate their characters, they need to be able to manipulate their audience.

ALAN ~

Writers need to be able to manipulate their audience.

I believe that is impossible, Julie. The thrust of Jim's thesis is to adjust your work to satisfy the audience -- not to transform ("manipulate") them.

When I work as a salesperson I have to make my clients like me.

That's why you're having trouble selling scripts. You've been a member of Zoetrope for 12 years, with 187 reviews and 42 screenplay submissions. The problem is not opportunity or industry or personal charm. What's stopping you from success is the belief that you can manipulate an outcome by using psychological tricks.

Nothing you can do or say in person, or in a cover letter, or a phone call ("emotionally connect with them") will influence a reader's experience or an audience watching a movie. Forget whatever Zoe reviewers say. Most of the time, it's a meaningless social game, where personalities and ruffled feathers are in play.

The B List is a little different. We like to be helpful and candid -- but only pertaining to the work of writing and rarely (if ever) to the personhood of the writer. For your own sake, you should be anonymous as a writer. No more penis jokes or "raging maniac" manipulation. It won't alter the script you wrote, and saying how passionate you are about the story won't make pro readers feel anything. They don't care who wrote what or why.

What matters here is story. Only story. Never anything other than story, the thing that studio readers and agents and producers read. I've stressed the importance of small cast and straight storytelling. Kalergis is right about high concept audience bonding.

You don't have to write that way to succeed. There's not much wrong with [your current project]. Submit it to someone who makes that kind of film, without trying to twist their arm off. You can't manipulate the audience, except in the technical sense of unexpected and sudden reversal of fortune that Lucy mentioned [in another thread] which works only once or twice in a movie. Uncle Billy loses a bank deposit / George Bailey is saved by Clarence the angel.

I'm opposed to flashbacks on principle for two reasons, and the first of these is "manipulation." Flashbacks ask us to suspend disbelief again for educational purposes. Worse: it breaks unfolding story continuity. We're supposed to write screenplays in the present tense (he goes to fight, she screams, he ignores her) and stay in the present tense from beginning to end.

The reader's minds-eye conjures a movie when reading your script. No awareness of you the writer, unless the script pulls tricks to "manipulate" an emotional response, which always fall flat. I'm not talking about your work in particular. I'm stating a general principle. Tell the story. What happens? and then what? -- in realistic or fanciful progress of an entertaining ride.

JULIE ANN ~

Manipulation and Art are blood brothers. When you walk into an art gallery and see a painting with a woman holding her head in her hands, the artist wants to manipulate his audience into feeling something -- anything. I may look at it and laugh. You may look at it and cover your eyes, but the manipulation is still there, whether we want to accept it or not.

JIM ~

Artists seek to capture the attention of their audience and elicit an emotional response, but I don't think "manipulate" is the right word to describe what they're doing. Manipulate, when used in the sense of controlling another person, implies sinister or devious intent, like a kid who manipulates a parent. When the word "manipulate" is used in the context of controlling inanimate things, such as a tool or piece of machinery, there is no sinister or devious intent implied. In that respect, the word's a little tricky, because its meaning changes when used in the context of controlling other people.

ALAN ~

1,440 "paintings" on each 1-minute script page (about 7 per word)

Fifteen seconds (1/4 page) feels like an eternity if nothing happens.

JULIE ANN ~

I like the word manipulate. I think humans have cast a dark shadow upon it because no one likes to think they can be manipulated into doing something they wouldn't normally do.

ALAN ~

I just opened a single serving of applesauce. The label said applesauce. Currently eating confident that it's made entirely from apples and nothing else.

Everything we do in film is a product. I must have heard that 100 times as a director on projects of all sizes: "Bring me finished product!" Products have labels. Exhibitors and audiences want to know what it is.

THE PRODUCERS (farce)
GOVERNOR MIKE (political satire)
THE GODFATHER (mafia drama)
BODY DOUBLE (crime thriller)
STAR WARS (sci-fi adventure)

Forget loglines. What's the product in one or two words?

imdb.com/Sections/Keywords

BILL ~

I agree that 'manipulate' is open to misperception and I understand the distinction you are making, Jim, but I thought originally that Julie used the word in the correct sense - at least I hope she did.

Manipulate is a transitive verb for which the 20 vol *OED* gives three meanings in this order:

> 1. To handle, esp. with dexterity; to manage, work, or treat by manual (and by extension, any mechanical) means.
> 2. To operate on with the mind or intelligence; to handle or treat (questions, artistic matter, resources etc.,) with skill.
> 3. To manage by dexterous contrivance or influence; esp to treat unfairly or insidiously for one's own advantage.

Clearly the only 'sinister or devious' interpretation is that of No. 3, but I understood originally Julie to be using the word in sense No. 2 - and that sense, as I see it, involves using all the techniques of audience/protag bonding that you have already discussed.

I also think that sense No. 2 chimes with Alan's insistence on story because constructing a good story involves using one's mind or intelligence to wrought the base material with skill -- and it should be remembered that the archaic verb 'wrought' is the root of the word 'wright', as used in the compound noun 'playwright', meaning a professional maker or author of plays, a dramatist, and which is effectively the root of the more modern term 'screenwriter.'

However, it now seems from Julie's further comment amplifying her original usage of the word 'manipulate' that she appears to be using it in sense No. 3, i.e. trying to control the audience for the writer's benefit. That technique for a plastic artist -- and Julie did speak about walking into an art gallery -- generally fails as the audience generally perceives (often on an unconscious level) that the artist is trying to manipulate them to hide the superficiality and banality of their work. I also suggest that that approach also fails for a playwright or screenwriter too. Film audiences are not stupid and their collective emotional responses are actually quite sophisticated; any whiff that they are being manipulated and they turn aggressively on the manipulator -- if only by panning the film and voting with their feet at the box office.

More important, in my opinion, than the foregoing objection to attempting to manipulate an audience in the sense of meaning No. 3 is that any script which aims to do so is not honest. True, there are many screenwriters who are not honest, yet this has not damaged their financial success -- it's also true of plastic artists -- and those who wish to emulate them are welcome to do so. Nevertheless, I think that success in any field of human endeavour that is not built on personal integrity and intellectual honesty is not worth having. Unfortunately, there seems to be few around who share my view, though I think that some here in The B List do (which is why I spend so much time here).

ALAN ~

Returning to something Jim said:

> Artists seek to capture the attention of their audience
> and elicit an emotional response

Speaking for myself and certain painters, sculptors and musicians of my aquaintance, the pursuit of conceiving and composing a work of great beauty or personal expression is an end in itself. Has nothing to do with an audience.

Mozart wrote church music as "work-for-hire"

Mozart's response to the idea of making church music was a little like the average child's reaction to being told to eat his spinach. While employed in Salzburg, Mozart wrote a dozen masses. And even after he escaped to Vienna and was free to write whatever he wanted, he began work on another religious work. [NPR]

As screenwriters, the vital career move is work-for-hire assignments and effective collaboration with producers. We write saleable stories for the canon of bankable audience expectation (not unlike Mozart eating his spinach). Those journeyman work habits and creative constraints are not dissimilar to a craft guild. If you write for television, there is a series Bible that dictates what you can and cannot do with characters and plot. No different than a priest or vicar forbidden to contradict their equally obligatory Bible, because it would upset audience expectations.

With a spec script, you're free to create whatever beauty and agony you see as an original work of art for the screen. These unborrowed stories and unforced vision move the world forward.

JULIE ANN ~

Thanks, Bill that is exactly how I meant the word to be translated.

In the novel *Control*, Germany gains control of Americans by providing them with entertainment that demonstrates how wonderful and kind Germans are. After reading that novel, I realized how often I have been manipulated by everything I see, touch or feel, that mankind created.

Do we have Pet stores because of Lassie? Or was Lassie invented because people love pets? Animals used to be required to serve some sort of purpose, now we have pets that live like kings; hell, there is even a new jacket to keep them from having panic attacks.

Novels, books, movies, TV shows changed the way we treat our pets.

The same can be said for spousal abuse, child abuse, etc. Artists have a strong need to change things for the better. Their inner theme, or heart of their creation pops up in everything they create. If it doesn't, it isn't art; it's just a thing that has no lasting value.

Alan I think you are wrong regarding how people feel about the artist. I just read Frankenstein for the first time. Knowing a little bit about Mary Shelley made the novel a lot more interesting because I could wonder whether or not her multiple miscarriages as well as still births inspired her to write Frankenstein.

BILL ~

Feminist critics for a generation or more have been saying that was her inspiration, but it was an unheard of view in my callow youth when I first read the book. I thought it was a poor read then and still do, but had I known what may have driven Mrs Shelley to write it I would not have changed my mind. In fact, I do not believe that one has to know anything about the artist for their work to speak to one, as the work should achieve that in and of itself in my opinion.

An example of what I mean is Vermeer's painting 'The Milkmaid' which Alan has just posted. When I first saw that -- again in my callow youth -- I knew nothing about the artist or his influences, but was drawn to the wondrous quality of the light and the masterful exquisiteness of the execution. In fact, had I been told beforehand Vermeer's life story and influences it would not have added anything to my sheer engagement and enjoyment of the painting. The art alone spoke for itself.

Part Two

Undeserved Misfortune

JIM ~

AUDIENCE/PROTAG BONDING – The "Connection Factor" Part 2

In Part 1, we looked at the importance of the connection factor, and why without it we're dead at the getgo. In Part 2, we'll look at techniques for causing the audience to connect with our protagonist and the theory behind those techniques.

The first task in establishing the audience/protag connection is getting the audience to accept the protagonist as a living, breathing human being… like them. The techniques for accomplishing this task are simple enough:

<u>Have your protagonist experience emotional reactions and physical sensations that the audience has experienced and therefore can relate to.</u>

One could argue that the ability to experience or feel things on a physical and emotional level is what separates the animate (life) from the inanimate. (everything else) Thus, if within the context of our setup, we cause our protag to experience or feel things, we make them more human in the eyes of our audience.

Examples of physical sensations that everyone has experienced at one time or another:

PAIN – A paper cut, a toothache, a blow, a fall, a sunburn, any physical injury no matter how small.

DISCOMFORT – Caught in the rain with no coat, new shoes that don't fit, a rash, too hot or cold, as in blistering heat or a sub-zero winter.

Examples of emotional reactions that everyone has experienced at one time or another:

FEAR – By reason of a real or imagined threat

LOSS – Of anything from car keys to a pet, to a loved one.

ANXIETY OR NERVOUSNESS – In reaction to a perceived threat to their status quo or self-image.

SELF-DOUBT OR SHYNESS – When challenged by events to grow in some way.

LOVE/HATE, LIKES/DISLIKES – The protag loves his dog and hates brussel sprouts.

Another way to make your protag more human:

Endow your protag with character traits that exemplify, at least in the minds of others, what it means to be "an honorable human being" or to be "a real man."

Examples:

SELF-SACRIFICE – Puts own interests on the line for the good of another or others. Anything from diving on a grenade to offering one's coat to a stranger.

PERSONAL INTEGRITY – Stands up for self and own beliefs. Doesn't cave in when faced with a dilemma that might require compromise of ones own principles.

PERSISTANCE – Doesn't give up.

NEGATIVE TRAITS – In some cases a negative trait can enhance connection, while at the same time giving the character room to arc.

Once the audience/reader accepts your protag as human, the next task is to create the connection -- get them to bond.

First the theory behind the approach…

Sadly we don't live in a fair world, and we never will. Bad things happen to good people. Good things happen to bad people. Random, weird, and even insane things happen for no discernable reason. Audiences and readers, try as they might, cannot deny that the above is observably true in real life.

But in story worlds, audiences and readers insist on fairness… good things come to those who wait… what comes around goes around… all effects have logical causes. They fully expect that everyone, particularly the protag and the antag, will get what's coming to them. In fact they will root for that end, and if we as writers don't give it to them they become seriously pissed. I still haven't forgiven Aaron Sorkin for killing off Miss Landingham in the West Wing series!

The audience/reader craves a story world that's fair. One that in the end balances the scales of justice. Let's call this factor, "karma balance."

SCENARIO #1

Johnny is a rich kid. He's led a pampered life. He works hard, gets great grades, goes to an Ivy League school, overcomes lots of obstacles and goes on to become a high paid exec in his father's company.

SCENARIO #2

Young Johnny through no fault of his own becomes homeless. Not only did he lose his real loving dad at a young age, but he got in his place a drunken stepfather who routinely beat the crap out of him. When he protested the stepdad kicking his dog, he was beaten and thrown out on the street. He and his little dog are now on their own. Johnny's a really smart, good kid, and somehow he manages to fend for himself and not become part of the foster home system. He even manages to get a part-time job despite being underage. In this story of remarkable struggle, the boy manages to overcome incredible obstacles, get though college, get a job, and eventually become a mover and shaker who endows a charity for abused and abandoned children.

In which of the above scenarios would you be more likely to connect with and root for the protagonist? No contest, right?

The key is that in the second scenario, we threw Johnny's "karma balance factor" way out of balance.

Undeserved misfortune!

That's the entirety of the technique.

In the scenario 2, we loaded up our protagonist with undeserved misfortune:

Lost his dad
Got an evil stepdad.
Suffered physical and emotional abuse.
Became homeless while still in his teens.

Man, is this kid's karma out of balance or what?!

Being a screenwriter is in many respects akin to being a stage magician. If the audience catches us in our trickery, there will be no applause. So we must write this character well enough that the audience buys him, not seeing the man behind the curtain, so that they can't help but connect. Their human need/desire for "karma balance" compels them. That much undeserved misfortune in the beginning of the tale MUST be offset by a positive win at the end of the tale and the audience gets entirely behind the protag in his efforts to achieve that end.

The same technique applies to the antagonist, who goes out of karma balance in the other direction. The audience can't wait to see them get theirs!

It takes considerable skill to integrate these techniques seamlessly into a story, but after a while it comes naturally. Most scripts by newcomers never get past the first step, making the protag human. Knowing and using these techniques can make a world of difference in how well your work is received by readers. Give it a try.

To my knowledge, these techniques have not been previously codified. But even a casual look at successful films reveals how commonly these techniques are used. My guess is that many good storytellers have learned them without ever recognizing exactly how they worked. Natural storytellers seem to use them instinctively.

Hope this makes sense to y'all.

ALAN ~

> *PAIN*
> *DISCOMFORT*
> *FEAR*
> *LOSS*
> *ANXIETY*
> *SHYNESS*
> *LOVE/HATE*

Immediately thought of The Flight of the Phoenix (1965)

> *The audience craves a story world that's fair*

Oh my god...

Charlton Heston (Moses) parting the Red Sea
Yul Brynner (Pharoah) defeated and destroyed

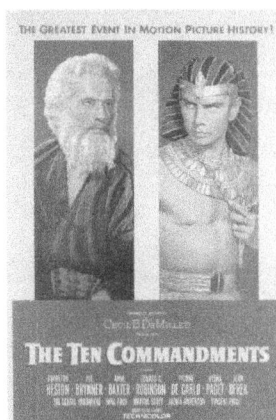

RLB ~

I don't think he means that characters are treated fairly by the world. ;)

ALAN ~

In act one, Pharoah has absolute power.

New thought. Alejandro taught me that the first shot is the most important shot in the movie. By extension, the first scene... our first glimpse of the protaganist. (In theater, protagonist: "appears first")

This is the 1st shot of DeMille's TEN COMMANDMENTS

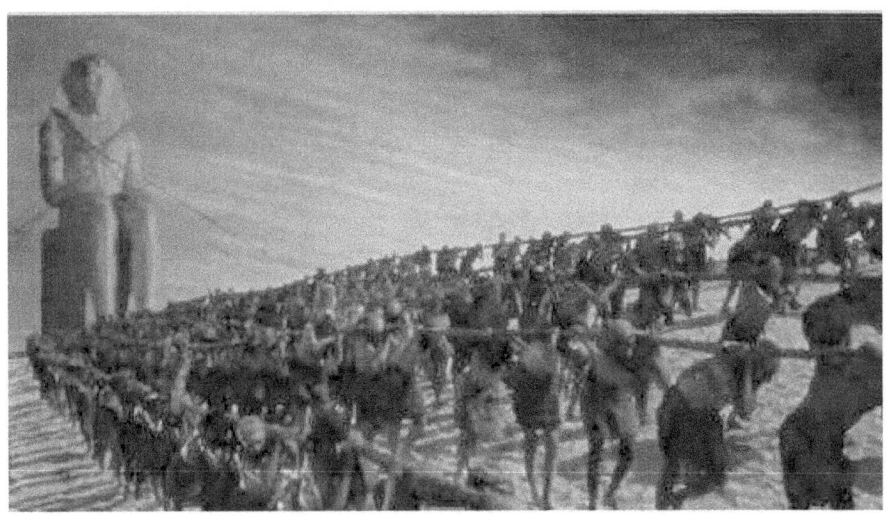

Undeserved misfortune indeed!

p.s. - a little homage to C.B. in the Short Stories wing uploaded just now. Also here in the Office Files.

ROB ~

OUTSTANDING! I think I'm going to move into Jimmy K's house and just look over his shoulder. Tell your wife that I cook, Jim.

BILL ~

Jim,

Thank you for this masterful summary. Whist everything you say is valuable, I particularly like the images this part conjured up in my head (no pun intended):

> Being a screenwriter is in many respects akin to being a stage magician. If the audience catches us in our trickery, there will be no applause. So we must write this character well enough that the audience buys him, not seeing the man behind the curtain...

How true that is. Audiences come to the movie theatre expecting to have their emotions manipulated, but if that manipulation is too obvious, crude or preachy it spoils the whole illusion and ruins the audiences' desired effect.

As for your comment that "To my knowledge these techniques have not been previously codified," I believe that you are correct. In fact the only book that I've read which investigated the subject reasonably thoroughly is a 2003 academic work by Greg M. Smith entitled Film Structure and the Emotion System, which I can recommend as an interesting read, by the way. In the beginning, Smith says something which chimes with your exposition here:

> ...although almost everyone agrees that eliciting emotions is a primary concern for most films. In the modern world's emotional landscape, the movie theater occupies a central place: it is one of the predominant spaces where many societies gather to express and experience emotion.

The cinema offers complex and varied experiences; for most people, however, it is a place to feel something. The dependability of movies to provide emotional experiences for diverse audiences lies at the center of the medium's appeal and power.

I also agree with your statement: "My guess is that many good storytellers have learned [these techniques] without ever recognizing exactly how they worked. Natural storytellers seem to use them instinctively." My only wish is that I was one of that selective band.

ALAN ~

I got to thinking about one-sheet images, and how they put across the bonding gestalt.

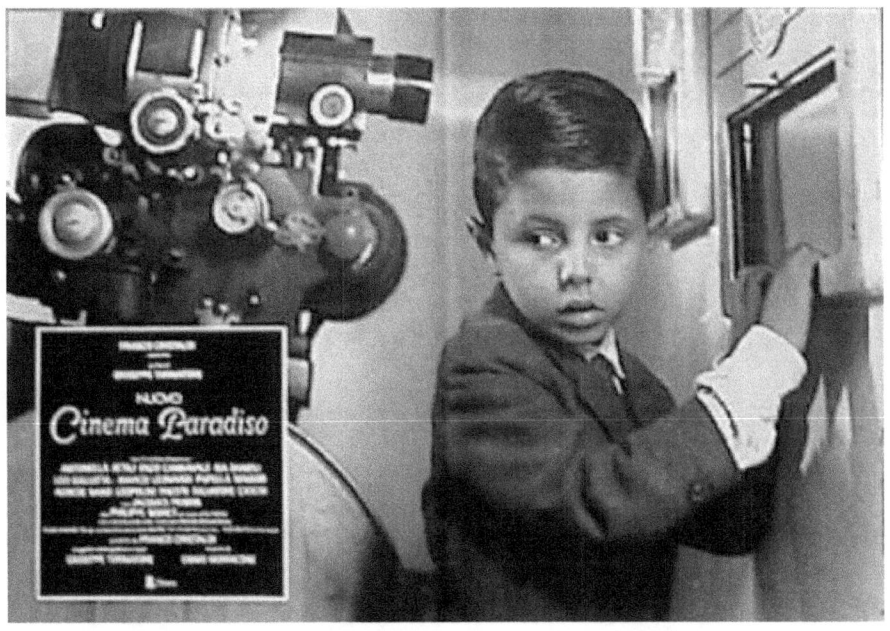

JIM ~

You're welcome, Bill.

When I hear the phrase "natural storyteller" I think of S.E. Hinton, who wrote the juvenile classic, THE OUTSIDERS, when she was a mere fifteen years old. FFC's film adaptation is true to the book.

The only natural storyteller I ever ran across was a kid who hired me to do a full analysis of his first screenplay. Format and presentation were the pits. Description was way overdone. Yet the story stayed with me for months.

Maybe I'll write a "part 3" examining THE OUTSIDERS in terms of the techniques described in part 2. That would probably only be worth the effort if you and other B-Listers have read the book or seen the film.

Alternatively, it might be an interesting experiment for B-Listers to watch THE OUTSIDERS individually and then point out the bonding techniques S.E. used so effectively. What do you think?

In my studies I never ran across "Film Structure and the Emotion System." I'll have to check it out. Thanks!

[to Alan] Got me thinking...

Do you think a brilliant actor can create the bonding effect by their presence alone?

ALAN ~

Depends on the first scene and throughline.

Mark Hamill as "Luke Skywalker" in STAR WARS. Not talking about the sequel franchise. Boychild, orphan, gentle, innocent, courageous.

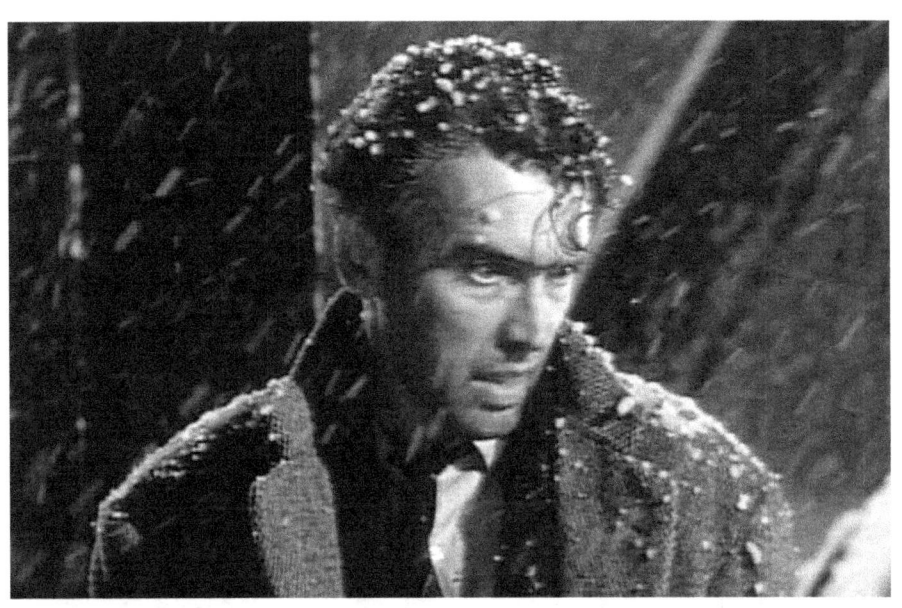

Jimmy Stewart carried WONDERFUL LIFE, MR SMITH GOES TO WASHINGTON, REAR WINDOW, ANATOMY OF A MURDER

"Americans liked Ronald Reagan as President of the United States, but were a little disappointed they couldn't get Jimmy Stewart."

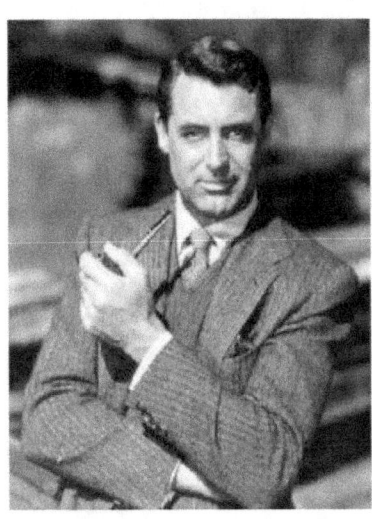

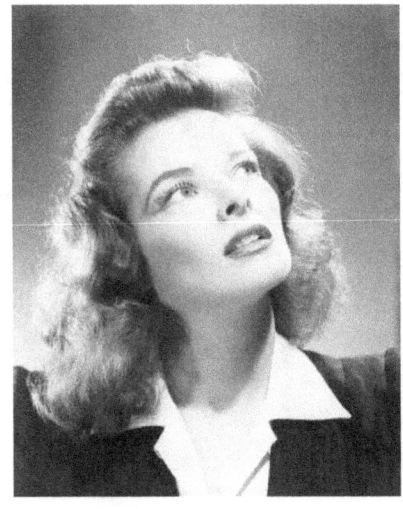

BILL ~

Maybe I'll write a "part 3" examining THE OUTSIDERS in terms of the techniques described in part 2. That would probably only be worth the effort if you and other B-Listers have read the book or seen the film.

I know the plot but haven't read the book or watched the movie. I do have access to a copy of the movie, however, and would watch it if sufficient numbers of others here were also going to do so to encourage you to make the effort to write Part 3.

ALAN ~

Do you think a brilliant actor can create the bonding effect...?

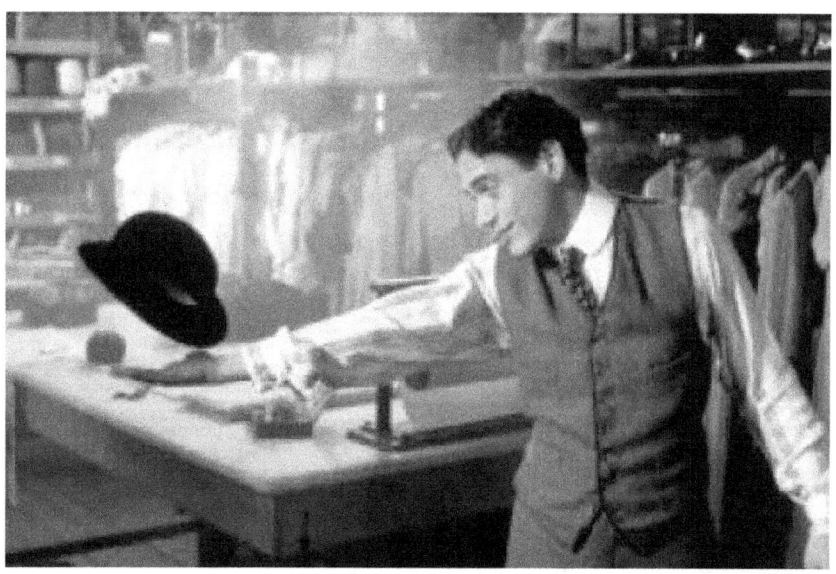

Robert Downey Jr. as Chaplin

Part Three

THE OUTSIDERS

JIM ~

S.E. Hinton wrote *The Outsiders* in her teens. To date, the book has sold over 16 million copies. Francis Ford Coppola made the movie in 1983.

At the time, Hinton was but a teenager. In my opinion, she's one of those rare birds, a natural storyteller.

Bill and I are going to watch the film, with my earlier post on audience bonding in mind, and then discus our observations. Anyone else want to play?

BILL ~

Well, I watched it last night, as I said I would. I was on the conscious look-out for all the 'audience bonding' techniques you mentioned in Part 2 of your essay, so I noticed them being used. Had I not been consciously studying the film, these technical details qua technical details would have passed unnoticed, though their bonding effect if I may call it that would still have worked on an emotional level. Every technique you mentioned in your essay was there, from fear, loss, etc., through to self-sacrifice, personal integrity and all the rest. An excellent lesson, Jim. Thank you for bringing it to my attention. More important, however, is to thank you for articulating the lessons so well.

When and if you ever get round to writing your book (what's keeping you, by the way?) I suggest you make 'audience bonding' your special take on how to write screenplays -- i.e. the thing which distinguishes your book from all the others on the subject -- and illustrate your points with appropriate movie references, such as The Outsiders.

Thanks again for a valuable and very important lesson.

JIM ~

You're very welcome, Bill.

I saw the film years ago, and so I gave it a fresh viewing last night. I was surprised by how many bonding elements were present in the storyline. It is a good case study.

I also found it interesting from a "karma balance" point of view. Johnny's death at the end of the film followed the principle, in that regardless of the circumstances, he did kill a boy in act 1.

I am actively working on a book between work that keeps the legal tender coming in. I think I'm looking at two books. Working titles:

SCREENWRITING FOR SMART PEOPLE

and

SCREEN STORY ANALYSIS

The first would be for writers and the second for writers, but also for readers, analysts, and others involved in the motion picture creative process.

I agree with you regarding approach. I've read maybe fifty books on the subject of screenwriting, and all but a few miss the mark, by not stressing the most basic underlying principles. An analogy would be books on motorcar design that go on and on about the trim, the fenders, interior lighting, etc,. and brush off information on how a drive train goes together.

ALAN ~

I like both titles and see why they're needed, especially a guide to Story Analysis for readers.

BILL ~

> *I also found it interesting from a "karma balance" point of view. Johnny's death at the end of the film followed the principle, in that regardless of the circumstances, he did kill a boy in act 1.*

Yes, you're correct, Jim, but I overlooked mentioning the principle which you had identified - Johnny had to pay for what he did, irrespective of his self-sacrifice re saving the kids, and the 'karmic balance', as you termed it, was restored with his death. Yet even his death was used to good effect - his references to Ponyboy's earlier recitation of Frost's poem etc. which propelled Ponyboy forward and endeared him (again) to the audience.

Re your further comment:

> *I am actively working on my book between work that keeps the legal tender coming in. I think I'm looking at two books - working titles:*
>
> *Screewriting for Smart People and Screen Story Analysis*
>
> *The first would be for writers and the second for writers, but also for readers, analysts, and others involved in the motion picture creative process.*

Two books would be an excellent idea, Jim. There appears to be a voracious market out there for anything on screenwriting per se, so the first title should sell well in its own right. However, I think that there is also a need for a work on screen story analysis too, as that would not only be useful for the wider market of those directly involved in the motion picture creative process but the millions in UK (and probably US) universities reading for a BA in film studies and the like.

Admittedly there are already a number of books with a similar thrust aimed at the academic market, but most I have encountered are more concerned with the author's waffling, rather than saying anything that is actually useful -- though *The Art of Watching Films (7th edition)* by Joseph M. Boggs & Dennis W. Petrie is a notable exception which I can recommend perusing. Another benefit of the academic market is that it tends to make for repeat sales, especially if the work becomes highly regarded (as I'm sure yours will).

Now please stop procrastinating and get on with it, so that I can buy your two books before I expire. On second thoughts, should I just send you the $20 now?

;-)

JULIE ANN ~

Jim, I haven't seen the film in years, but I felt an immediate connection with the characters because I could relate to them. They reminded my of my childhood friends, rebellious with only our conscience to guide us.

I had no idea the writer was in her teens when she wrote the book. You are right, she is a natural storyteller.

BILL (replying to Alan) ~

Very keen to see how discussion of OUTSIDERS evolves.

Yes, I would have liked more people to have joined it too -- as I'm sure would Jim -- but it doesn't look like anyone else is prepared to do so, though I can't imagine why, as there is much to learn from it thanks in particular to Jim's masterful summary of audience/protag bonding.

Incidentally, the movie was not the type of story I would usually watch so approached it as an academic exercise and tried to retain professional objectivity throughout. Despite my professional detachment, which enabled me to consciously identify all of the techniques Jim had explained in his article. I also found myself becoming involved on a subjective basis as an audience member, which rather proves the effectiveness of those professional techniques Jim identified for us.

JIM ~

Neither of us are the target audience for THE OUTSIDERS, but I recall seeing it upon first release and thinking it was a well done film.

One thing I've noticed about aspiring teen writers I've worked with, is that they tend to favor dark ending. That teen angst thing, I guess.

ALAN ~

En passant, an interesting film industry problem:

> *approached it as an academic exercise and tried to retain*
> *professional objectivity throughout*

The Academy members get mountains of "screeners" (formerly VHS cassettes, then DVDs) of movies nominated for a variety of reasons: Best Picture, Best Actor, Best Costumes, etc. Are they professionally objective while watching those films? Hell no. They watch a few and vote for friends.

However I'm thinking of something else. When I watch a film, it's a bad omen if I start seeing camera angles and in-shot camera moves, focus pull, lighting, coverage, wet streets, over-played bits and extras and long lenses. Parenthetically, that's why I always thought Woody Allen was a chump, Bob Zemeckis a show-off, and Robert Altman incompetent. From time to time I admire certain sequences, particularly production design. But nothing is quite so enjoyable as losing awareness of the nuts and bolts.

I think the right way to see a film objectively is to play it twice. Screen about 10 minutes without sound and see the movie. Rewind, turn the picture off and audition that same 10 minutes with sound only. Now you're ready to study the whole movie, aware of its visual "film form" and the aural/verbal "play" as distinct elements.

ROB ~

The more one knows about the tricks of the screenwriting and film-making trade, the more difficult it is to lose oneself and just enjoy a movie.

BILL ~

Good advice, Alan, but in my case I was specifically trying to watch the film objectively in order to see how the techniques Jim had delineated were used. In other words, I wanted to see the professional tricks, if you like, but subsequently found myself being sucked in emotionally due to the success with which they had been employed. Had I simply approached this film from an emotional standpoint -- i.e. not looking for the techniques Jim mentioned -- I wouldn't have bothered viewing it, as it was not my preferred type of story. But as Jim already said, geriatrics like me were not its intended audience. The interesting thing is that the techniques worked, nevertheless.

There's a valuable lesson there.

ROB ~

I know the more one knows about making a movie the better one becomes as a screenwriter.

There's been much discussion on how bad scripts can be, even recently on threads Julie Ann originated. I'd bet those writers who come out with crap don't know how movies are made.

Just MHO... the better the film, the more absorbed and lost in it I become.

RLB ~

When I was in college, I used to visit the juvenile room in the old library. One afternoon after class, I came across a copy of The Outsiders and read the entire book right there at the shelf, half standing up, the last half sitting on a footstool. Was late for supper, but it was worth it.

JIM ~

I read that The Outsiders still sells hundreds of thousands of copies a year.

RLB ~

When I learned how young the writer was, and how she had written her opus at her kitchen table, I was positively green with envy. By the time the movie was made and she'd written a couple other books, I was over it and able to fully appreciate her work.

Scene

Logic

Card

EXT. BOATHOUSE - DAY
Joanne, Fred

ESCAPE

Scene Cards

ALAN ~

Yep. Still hounding you to take this seriously. It matters and it works.

[compilation of three posts]

Let's say you have a first draft that runs 140 pages, or maybe the page count is okay, but a friend says: "You have too much movie."

Sometimes there's too much movie in two sentences:

> MOUNTAIN BLOWS UP, SINKS FLEET. JOE AND BETTY NARROWLY ESCAPE IN HOT AIR BALLOON AND THEY JOYOUSLY MAKE LOVE

A properly formatted page should run about 1 minute on the screen. If you're going to blow up a mountain and sink a fleet of ships, think about screen time. It usually takes at least 30 seconds (half a page of visuals) to blow up a mountain and destroy a fleet of ships. You have to write an action continuity. Tell us the story in pictures.

Throwaway dialogue doesn't show us pictures.

BETTY
E-e-e-e-e-k!

JOE
Hurry! This way!

SAILOR #1
(on fire)
A-i-i-i-i-i!

BETTY
Joe! Help me!

Okay, that was silly. Everybody knows that complex cataclysmic action needs a sequence of detailed action events on the page. The term *montage* means putting together. It's your job to put together an action sequence, bit by bit, indicating how much screen time it will require according to how much space it occupies on the page.

Supposing now that you're an expert at writing action and measuring the dialogue, so that every page times out at exactly 1 minute and the script is under 100 pages total -- you can still have too much movie if there are too many scenes and too many characters.

The rule of thumb is 40 scenes and 5 main characters.

I just finished reading a perfectly wonderful screenplay that had 72 scenes, not counting parallel action, with 7 or 8 main characters and a dozen supporting roles, not counting bit players (under-5's) and monsters. Too much movie.

HOW TO USE SCENE CARDS

Script doctors and experienced screenwriters use a simple method of analyzing what to do with too much movie. It helps trim an overweight first draft and highlights opportunities to tell a better story in rewrite.

Very simple method. You can do it in less than an hour.

Buy a pack of 3x5 cards. Go through your script page by page. Each scene is a new card. Write who, where, and what the essential action is in one verb.

```
EXT. BOATHOUSE - DAY
Joanne, Fred

          ESCAPE
```

If you have parallel action cross-cutting between two locales (each of which is a separate scene, of course) try to identify in each of them whether there is development internal to that locale. Example:

EXT. FRONT YARD - NIGHT

Billy

     BAFFLED

---------------------------- (intercut parallel action)

INT. BASEMENT - NIGHT

Donna and Monster

     FRANTIC

If Donna manages to kill the monster all by herself in the basement, then that development is a new 3rd scene, because she transcends her fear and summons her animal courage to CONQUER (a new action).

If you can't explain the essential action of a scene in one word, an action verb, then that scene probably doesn't belong in your movie. Scenes devoid of human action or purpose cannot be performed by actors. If Billy is BAFFLED (not an action verb; a static condition going nowhere), I'd cut it. Same thing with Donna's FRANTIC (not an action verb; a static condition; an adjective).

Movies should move. Characters seek, struggle, surmount, see, question, doubt, deny, refuse, play, joke, evade, caress, surrender, ponder, decide, destroy, search, laugh, cry, carry on, tire, fall asleep, wake up – all of which are action verbs – something to *do*.

Each scene should have an essential action to propel the story.

I understand that certain movies (ANNIE HALL) flail around doing little or nothing with pathetic characters who don't understand themselves and can't decide what to do, surrounded by other dysfunctional cripples and overbearing one-dimensional monsters.

Scene Cards can't help you do nothing. They force you to make movies that move, by asking "What is this scene about in one word?" and no two scenes should do the same thing.

Here I will insert something I that wrote a long time ago, recalling my mentor, the late Alejandro Rey, who explained how a professional actor prepares:

> I take the script one page at a time. On the blank side of the sheet, I divide into three columns. Actions, adjustments, activities. Now, what is this scene about? No, no. Too many words. Tell me what this scene is about in one word.

Very well. Now you have 60 or 70 cards, one for each scene. The next part of the process is stunningly simple. You shuffle them like playing cards and throw them into the air, landing on your living room floor in a confused mess, some of them upside down, your entire movie out of order and randomized.

Pick up each card, one at a time, look at the action word and decide afresh if it belongs in the First Act, Second Act, or Third Act. Sort the cards into three piles accordingly. Then take one pile and think through how that Act should be organized in progressive scene-actions.

Alejandro again:

> Before you write, you must think of scenes. The scenes. Here, tell me each scene you have planned. On the card I only write the characters' names, the place, and the action — in one word. What is the next? — And the next? — Now, look, is it better that he fights, he goes away, he feels

ashamed, he has hope? Or maybe that he has hope, he fights, and he feels ashamed? By moving the cards you can try many, many ideas — then you write.

Or rewrite. I've doctored a lot of scripts with Scene Cards, which usually drove screenwriters absolutely nuts, because I was a mad scientist mutilating their Baby, chopping off arms and legs and extra noses, which is probably true of every script. You have at least one extra nose somewhere in your screenplay, a scene that repeats an identical action. You don't need to do anything twice in a movie. One FALLS ASLEEP is enough. One LAUGHS is plenty.

Which raises another interesting matter revealed by Scene Cards. If you don't have a scene that LAUGHS, why not? Laughing at danger is the hallmark of a hero or heroine. Scene Cards help you rethink the vital goal of each scene and how to craft it. Anything that doesn't advance the essential action of that scene should be cut.

Anyway, the process of re-assembling the First Act, Second Act, Third Act (separate piles dealt with individually) forces you to honor George M. Cohan's architecture for a good play. In the first act, get your man up a tree. In the second act, throw stones at him. In the third act, get him down.

While we're at it, let's consult Buster Keaton:

Somebody would come up with an idea. "Here's a good start," we'd say. We skip the middle. We never paid any attention to the middle. We immediately went to the finish. We worked on the finish and if we get a finish that we're all satisfied with, then we'll go back and work on the middle. For some reason, the middle always took care of itself.

Thank you for plodding through my explanation of Scene Cards. Throwing your movie in the air, sorting it into three Acts with special attention to the beginning and the end, removing redundant scenes or whole sequences, and puzzling about what action is missing or unclear will illuminate the task of rewrite and help you trim "too much movie."

Do I really, really need that scene?

Very important. Making notes on the margin or screenwriting software doesn't cut it. You have to use stupid 3x5 cards, so you can shuffle the movie, throw it in the air and make a gigantic mess on the floor, scenes randomized out of order.

The crucial idea is to consider each scene out of sequence all by itself, like a short film. Each scene needs a beginning-middle-end and an arc of development internal to that scene. One character needs to own it.

The action verb is what that mini-movie is about.

When you assemble three cards (scenes) in a sequence, there is another beginning-middle-end among them. Those three scenes should tell a coherent story, without knowing anything else that (originally) came before or after that sequence. Small coherent sequences have enormous power and clarity.

Forget the movie you wrote. This is not about the movie you wrote. It's about individual scenes and sequences.

Do not hold the pack of cards, ever. Pushpin or Scotch tape them to a wall, with three big vertical stripes in masking tape to segregate Act One, Act Two, Act Three. If you don't have blank wall space and/or don't want a bunch of pushpin holes in it, buy a sheet of gypsum board or plywood and lean it against the wall.

This is not meant to be amusing. I am trying to convey to you the correct procedure of using Scene Cards. Sorting scenes into three piles First/Second/Third Act is fairly simple, but you have to deal with each Act separately (not sequentially). Putting together a sequence of three or four scenes is the way to start. No cheating. Get tough. If a card doesn't have a meaningful story action (verb), throw it aside and forget about it. Work with the meaty scenes that are vital to your story. Maximum 15 cards per Act. Vignettes and short parallel action cutaways should end up in a "maybe" pile.

To make it crystal clear that a scene is continuous action at one place, not two places or eleven places intercut, please consider this as-shot breakdown from Dreamworks' HOW TO TRAIN YOUR DRAGON. Give particular attention to scene lengths.

Sc.1 LONG SHOTS TO ESTABLISH ISLAND - NIGHT (30 seconds)

Sc.2 EXT. VILLAGE - NIGHT ... dragon battle action (1:15)

Sc.3 INT. WORKSHOP .. Hiccup wants to join the battle (25 seconds)

Sc.4 EXT. VILLAGE .. dragon battle continues (35 seconds)

Sc.5 INT. WORKSHOP .. Hiccup argues with his boss (1:00)

Sc.6 EXT. VILLAGE .. dragon battle continues (1:00)

Sc.7 INT. WORKSHOP .. Hiccup ordered to stay put (15 seconds)

Sc.8 EXT. VILLAGE .. Hiccup joins battle, has to be rescued (3:20)

Sc.9 EXT. WORKSHOP .. Hiccup despairs of failure (40 seconds)

Thus far, all of the action took place in strict continuity at one locale, cutting between EXT VILLAGE and INT WORKSHOP from which we can see continuous action. No doubt about where we are. No jump in time or place.

Total sequence: 9 minutes (9 pages) of action and dialogue, average scene length 1 minute.

Now, watch what's next:

Sc.10 INT. WAR ROOM .. Hiccup's father moans about him (2:00)

Sc.11 EXT. FOREST - DAY .. Hiccup finds Toothless (2:40)

The excitement and spectacle of the opening sequence gives way to story development. Longer scenes.

Later, there will be a long sequence in the Forest, where Hiccup learns to understand Toothless and slowly wins the dragon's confidence, ultimately fitting a prosthesis to his tail so he can fly again with Hiccup riding on his back. Very very long scenes, all in one location, just Hiccup and Toothless. I'll discuss two of those scenes.

Count each scene separately, because there is passage of time.

Sc.19 EXT. FOREST - DAY .. Hiccup brings a fish.

Sc.20 EXT. FOREST - DAY .. (later, lengthening shadows) Hiccup uses a stick to draw an image of Toothless in the sand. Toothless rips a sapling from the ground and drags it to make a strange maze of circles in sand, which Hiccup has to walk through without touching the lines. Toothless finally allows Hiccup to touch his nose, eyes closed, then stomps away grumpy.

Running time of those two scenes? 6 minutes (6 pages)

It doesn't matter whether you're writing mystery, action adventure, comedy, sci-fi, horror, or PG-rated animation. Pace is vital. It is measured in scenes and scene length.

ROB ~

Outstanding advice, Alan.

For one birthday, I bought three cork boards on a frame and wheels … act 1-2-3. Then I did the cards. It got me so objective to the story. It was magical.

JULIE ANN ~

Alan, my dyslexic brain had a hard time digesting directions. Could you do me a favor, when you have the time, and show me what the scene cards would look like for the first few scenes in "Licorice." Once I see how you did it with something I have written, I should be able to do the rest.

ALAN ~

Well, it's really for you to say what each scene is about. But I'll try.

Ext Meadow Day
James

... **CRUSH (HIMSELF)**

Ext Alexander Backyard Day
Heather

... **DISCOVER**

Int Alexander Kitchen Day
Heather, Bonnie, Carson

... **INSIST**

Ext Alexander Backyard
James, Bonnie, Carson, Heather

... **COLLAPSE**

Ext Cemetary Day
James, **Bonnie**, Heather, Carson

... **GRIEVE**

Int Brown's Office Day
Bonnie, Carson, **Dr Brown**

... **EXPLAIN**

Int Alexander Kitchen Night
James, Bonnie, **Carson**

... **COMMAND**

Int Bedroom Night
Bonnie, Carson

... **RESPOND**

Int Living Room Night
Kandice, David, Mrs Pollick,
Bonnie, Carson

... **DEFEND**

Int Hallway Night
Carson, James (O.S.)

... **BEG**

```
-------------------------------
```
Int Living Room Night
Heather, Kandice, David
Mrs Pollick, Bonnie

... **ENJOY**

```
-------------------------------
```

In each scene I **bolded** the character who I thought owned the scene and carried it dramatically.

JULIE ~

Thanks Alan, now I need to make a copy of what you did and see if I can find the same emotions.

ALAN ~

Not emotions. Actions. Things that actors *do* and *perform*.

JULIE ANN ~

That would explain why I am confused :)

SALLY ~

Here's a link to an article by Alex Epstein that might help you: _Verbs._ Epstein is talking about finding the action verb that drives a piece of dialogue, as an actor or a writer. As I understand Alan he's taking the same concept and applying it to the scene level: *What is the action verb that is driving this scene?* -- Alan, am I on the right track here?

ALAN ~

Yes. Movies should move.

A little further discussion about this. We too often ask actors to *do* and *perform* the impossible, like portray inner states, complex thoughts, ambiguity and perplexity.

Take confusion for example. The only way to portray confusion is a rapid series of wrong guesses and then freeze. Good reference is George C. Scott's performance in the 3rd act of DOCTOR STRANGE-LOVE, in shirtsleeves, no decorum or composure left as an Air Force general officer, baffled, suspicious, sly, proud, silly, triumphant, and aghast -- all in 15 seconds.

Comedy doesn't obey the usual rules of drama, but Scott's scene was his to carry and his performance worked because he made it move in quick nimble pieces to convey the goal of that scene: **SELF-IMPEACH (**to **REVEAL** his adolescent idiocy and uselessness).

JULIE ANN ~

If a script should only have 40 scenes, my script, "Licorice" is already in trouble because I have used up eight in the first seven pages.

ALAN ~

Well, yes, that's something to consider. I usually say that the thing to concentrate on, in developing a screenplay, are the big meaty 4-page scenes (if any). I understand that things have changed in recent years, and I'm an old fashioned troglodyte, but the central question for me is production cost.

Set-ups are not as simple as picking up the camera and going somewhere else. Day exteriors are usually too "hard" to point and shoot, so we use scrims on hi-lifters and 9-lights for fill. Interiors are worse. That's why the number of scenes becomes important -- unless most of them are on sound stage sets. Movies are shot out of sequence. Set up and do all the Living Room scenes, then all the Bedroom scenes, then all the Kitchen scenes, etc.

However (and it's a big however), when you're writing something you care about, go ahead and write the movie you see in your head. It might have to be rewritten and doctored for production cost later if it's sold to a producer who has to make the movie on a shoestring budget of $2-3 million.

SALLY ~

By 40 scenes, do you mean 40 sluglines, or 40 sequences?

JULIE ANN ~

Alan broke my script up by the master scenes. According to McKee, a scene can take place in a different location so long as the action remains continuous.

ALAN ~

According to McKee a scene can take place in a different location so long as the action remains continuous

I never understood what that meant. A scene is continuous action in one place, period. We can fudge a little around the edges, especially if there's a standing set with two or three adjoining rooms, but that pertains only to studio projects -- not low budget indie pix shot on location.

In a previous discussion of Scene Cards, I said:

… a scene is uninterrupted continuous action in one place, without cutting to another time or place. Film crews have to assemble every-thing required to stage and photograph that scene. Two scenes shot on the same set might be completely different: Day, night, cast, wardrobe, etc. Scenes are what actors rehearse, directors direct, and production managers endeavor to shoot out-of-sequence to maximize unit efficiency.

<u>Day 5, Stage 4, 8:00 a.m. Call</u>

Sc.12 INT - DAY - ATTIC
Sc.38 INT - NIGHT - ATTIC ON FIRE
Sc.40 INT - DAY - ATTIC SCORCHED

Standby painters and decorators are there to rapidly re-dress the set when Sc. 12 is in the can. Fire is done with propane. They can 'burn' the set repeatedly. Day and Night are simple lighting changes. Two actors appear in the first scene; a stunt double in the fire scene; three other actors investigate the scorched attic. All of them have to be on set when needed in costume and make-up/hair. All three scenes are shot in one 10-hour day.

"Scene" comes to us from the legitimate stage, the root source of cinematic staging, acting, directing, dance, set design and special effects (wind, rain, snow, forced perspective). In the early days of filmmaking all actors and directors came from Broadway. Stage scenery is a physical set-up. Scenes are separated by a 'black-out' or curtain drawn across the stage to conceal movement of sets, back-grounds, and props being changed for a new scene.

It's an important part of the job of screenwriting to be aware of how movies are made. The cast and crew go somewhere (a room, a street, a car in traffic) and spends hours to dress the locale and light it. Then there's a walkthrough. When it's time to shoot that scene, it's covered from several angles by setting and resetting the camera, which always necessitates some lighting changes. Takes hours to do a single scene. Film crews can't hop around like frogs.

40 scenes sounds skimpy or niggardly until you try to make a 35mm feature film on less than $2 million. The Brits and Europeans use 16mm and pay everybody slightly less, to rachet their "negative cost" of a TV feature down to $1 million. That's why cheap movies are claustrophobic and talky – almost like soap operas.

It would be nice to write a big $40 million script and sell it for a $500,000 payday. Story development is usually 5% of budget. Very very very few writers make that kind of money. Guild minimum is less than $30,000. I made that twice in my career (also made money directing, but that's not germane to discussing screenwriting per se).

Folks who are trying to write their way in should have modest expectations about what they will be paid for original story, screen-play, and two rewrites to the producer's satisfaction. $50,000 is a lot of money. And the fastest way to earn it is to write something that's easy and cheap to produce.

40 scenes, 5 main characters, no fancy props or fx.

SALLY ~

Thank you for the clarification, Alan.

> *40 scenes sounds skimpy or niggardly until you try to make a 35mm feature film on less than $2 million. The Brits and Europeans use 16mm and pay everybody slightly less, to rachet their "negative cost" of a TV feature down to $1 million. That's why cheap movies are claustrophobic and talky – almost like soap operas.*

Funny. I've been watching The Sandbaggers, a British TV spy series from the late 70's. It is *very* claustrophobic and talky. And yet, the writing is so superb, the shows are still highly watchable and enjoy-able today.

I'll go for low budget + good writing / storytelling over costumes and locations and FX any day.

ROB ~

Tremendous post, Alan. I love McKee, but he's really hard to understand. You make it easier.

JIM ~

*"According to McKee a scene can take place in a different
location so long as the action remains continuous."*

McKee is the king of over-complications. He could give a three-hour
lecture on how to erase a blackboard.

ROB ~

That's hilarious, Jim, but so true.

JIM (to another poster) ~

*"McKee has a different definition of scene from what Alan is
offering and I'm not at a level to say which one is right."*

Go with Alan. His is the voice of experience. To define the word scene
in the context of a screenplay as per McKee leads to confusion as to
when new scene headings are required. If McKee's scene theory helps
you, that's great, but go with Alan's in practice. At least that's my take
on it.

There's a lot we can learn from McKee and the other gurus, but it's a
HUGE mistake to accept all their pronouncements as truisms. While
much of what they have to say is of value, there's also a good portion
of what they teach that is absolute crap. The test is: Does the insight
or teaching point in question make you a better writer? Does it have
application in the real world? Is it really a universal truth, or is it a
hobby horse?

ALAN ~

McKee suggested we light an entire house and garage, for what purpose? And how credible is 'I love you' in the morning, if it collapses five minutes later?

His positive and negative charges are soap opera rubbish.

Explicit and fundamental in the Scene Card theory of story is the idea of action. Something an actor **does**. It can be simple (DECEIVE). It can be complicated (SEDUCE). The action of the scene is carried by someone in particular, not an ensemble.

In McKee's example of a woman and a man, one of them must carry the scene. Suppose she has a secret, established in a previous scene, I hope. He finds out somehow, confronts her, gets another tissue of dissembling lies, storms out angrily. What's the action? Not betrayal. Not his discovery of betrayal. Not the hollow attempt to cover it up and explain it away.

That scene is about DIVORCE, and it's *his* scene to carry, whether it results in a phone call to his attorney later on or never. Divorce is the price of betrayal, unless he BETRAYS HIMSELF by caving in, turning the car around and wimpily asks her to forgive him for getting angry about being betrayed and lied to.

There is no "positive" or "negative" unless you consider the man's moral integrity and the meaning of marriage. If he walks out, never to return, after being betrayed and lied to – okay, I suppose that's a positive affirmation of his moral integrity. Fat lot of good it will do him in divorce court. It's a fucking disaster for all concerned. It's a deterrent to moral integrity, usually sufficient to try to patch things over and swallow his pride.

Switch the characters around. He betrayed her and got found out. Same result, except that *she* carries the scene. She has to *act*. Divorce or cave in?

ALAN (to a dissenter who declined to let us quote him) ~

It is not necessary to agree with me. But "action" sailed right past you, didn't mean a damn thing to you apparently.

Put yourself in the shoes of an actor. No matter what the script says, he has to come up with a concept of how to play the scene. Unless you the screenwriter put little plusses and minusses in front of each slug line, whenever you the screenwriter think things are supposed to change their "charge," the actor will use his own training and knowledge of his craft to interpret the scene. He might even improvise.

A scene can be played many ways.

Good directors don't hand out dog biscuits or lumps of coal. They encourage actors to find their own vision of what the scene is about (in one word). Once the actor has an essential action, he sculpts it with adjustments and activities ("business") which the director will perhaps trim a bit to accommodate the camera and perhaps stretch for dramatic pace.

You the screenwriter are not involved in shooting or performing your script.

What I have attempted to make clear is the practical business of staging and performing action that can be rendered on film. We do it one scene at a time.

Depending on your sense of story, it is conceivable that you might have a scene about nothing (AFTER THE FOX, 1966) or very little (THE BREAKFAST CLUB). It might be all stunt action (DRUNKEN MASTER II).

The proper goal of writing for the screen ought to be originality.

McKee cannot help you do that.

JIM (to a dissenter, who said) ~

"Don't confuse scenes with slug lines."

The word "slugline" is synonymous with "scene heading." Each new scene begins with a slugline.

SCENE HEADING... A short description of the location and time of day of a scene, also known as a slugline. For example EXT. MOUNTAIN CABIN - DAY would denote that the action takes place outside a mountain cabin during daylight hours. [www.playwriting101.com/glossary]

SCENE... Action taking place in one location and in a distinct time that (hopefully) moves the story to the next element of the story. [ibid]

The word scene can also mean a unit of drama. That's a more general definition, and it's McKee's use of the word. I can see that definition as appropriate when talking dramatic theory in general.

ALAN (after colloquy about a news item) ~

I don't think you understand. I turned drama into farce. This isn't an off-the-wall silliness. It is exactly what happened to Stanley Kubrick. A book he optioned in 1962 and his first draft script were extremely serious straight drama. The project had a "one sheet" and was slated for production. But it took so long for Kubrick and various creative partners to write and rewrite, that he got a little punch-drunk and started laughing at how absurd it all was. That's when he called in Terry Southern. The result was DOCTOR STRANGELOVE. Nor does my little homily end there. Much of Peter Sellers' dialogue in the dual role of President Muffley and of Dr. Strangelove was improvised on the set. Not performed as written, although the screenplay was hilarious and could have been performed as written.

Do you see? -- screenwriters are only partly involved in telling a story, staging it, interpreting it, covering it, and cutting it. The part you get to do is broad structure. Three acts. Beginning, middle, end.

If you dick around with subplots or flashbacks, it's harder to see the "throughline" as Jim would say.

Same thing with scenes. Give yourself 40. Let each one be **about something** expressed in dramatic action, no two alike. If your palette is binary (positive negative) you are excused from creating 40 unique scenes that unfold with the power of continuously expanding drama or farce, as the case may be.

BILL ~

I've followed you so far, Alan, but I am a little puzzled by your statement that one can exceed 40 scenes: *If [one's] palette is binary (positive negative) you are excused from creating 40 unique scenes...*

Would you care to elucidate, please?

ALAN ~

Good afternoon, Bill. I should probably give up the struggle. My goal was to tempt readers into writing standalone unique scenes, each one carried by a single character (sometimes him, sometimes her, a few by supporting cast or bit players). 40 or so is a good budget.

BILL ~

And Good Day to you, Alan.

I wasn't trying to beat you into submission, just hoping for some clarification, as I am keen to minimise anything which will make my screenplays less marketable. Hell, if I was any good at scriptwriting, I wouldn't need to pose questions here, because I'd be too busy hammering out my next mega-sale. Even a small sale at the UK equivalent of union rates would be good.

I should add that I find your lessons very useful -- but especially this scene card one -- and I am in the process of trying to apply them and the comments you made in your review of my script into the rewrite which is currently underway.

ALAN ~

You and I are on good terms, Bill. Actually I appreciate your support, questions, willingness to participate here. When Rob suggested that I write a book about screenwriting, my shoulders slumped. Not much of a writer. I started as a teen filmmaker. The entire focus of my career was directing.

I shouldn't be so petty about McKee. My view of scripts was shaped by experience. Nine times out of ten, they don't work on the set. Dialog sounds flat. It would nice if writers left some space for actors to breathe, react, think, paw around in the earth of a performance space.

What we use scripts for primarily is to mark up coverage (directors) and adjustments/activities (actors) on the opposite blank white back of the previous page. Story matters enormously, and it's ideal to have a straight, clear, understandable plot, because we always shoot out of sequence. No one has the luxury of making a movie Sc.1, Sc.2, Sc.3 etc. That's why asking ourselves in development and later in rehearsal on the set "What is this scene about?" becomes important. How do we convert the abstract dramatic action into marks, angles, camera movement?

Great actors have a tough job. Sir Larry was hopeless. He'd giggle, vomit, hide in the wings or in his trailer, forget his lines. Best actor that ever lived (KHARTOUM, 1966). Serviceable character actors are tradesmen. Spencer Tracy summed it up nicely, explaining his craft as: "Memorize your lines." Travolta, Willis, Cruise, Gibson, Stallone slid by on personality. Good enough for selling popcorn and putting bums on seats. No problem taking a script at face value, doing a workmanlike job. Plenty of time and money to stage complex scenes, shoot maybe a page a day.

What we (indies, new screenwriters) face is the nightmare of doing good work on poverty row B-picture budgets. Better scenes make it a joy. Gives actors a professional challenge, doesn't depend on a fat budget, big crew, a lot of difficult in-shot camera movement.

Sorry to blather. Not at my best this morning.

BILL ~

Not blather. Always thought-provoking. Ever interesting.
Sorry you don't feel bright-eyed and bushy-tailed this AM.
In the words of the sage: It will pass.
All the best, mate.

JIM ~

The problem I have with McKee's positive/negative thing is that upon inspection, many excellent scripts don't conform to this pattern. For example, toward the end of act two the pattern in a good script is often times: **Negative - more negative - more negative – gawd awful negative ("darkest hour").**

There are also expository scenes, and there are scenes for pacing or comic/dramatic relief where change is minimal.

ROB ~

McKee clarified some things for me and for that I'm grateful. But after years of studying and practicing, like I said and implied, rules (for me) cannot become fixed ideas.

I think (again for me) the three acts are important and along those lines, timing. Then I think it's important to know how to enter drama into the story. I think that's what McKee is saying when speaking of the positive vs the negative.

I agree with what you say, there can be something bad that happens, then another and another, on and on and at the end the protagonist is still breathing, barely = negative, negative, more negative and even more negative.

The drama may not occur till the next act.

His very thick book does make a great door stopper. I applaud what he's done, and I know many of his students have done well. Am I mistaken to say he hasn't written many scripts nor been on the big screen? I could be wrong. I think I'm going to IMDB him.

JULIE ANN ~

I appreciate what everyone is saying regarding scene cards, but I know I would hate creating a script that way; it's too restrictive. But I can see how they would help someone figure out what needs to be removed, or perhaps just moved to a different location.

ALAN ~

========= **THE CASE OF THE EMPTY CASE**, pp. 7-12 =========

EXT. BREMER BUILDING – DAY

Yellow taxi pulls up to the curb outside old brick office building at Hollywood & Highland.

Car door opens and CHRIS gets out, slams door, fumbles in his pockets for money.

TAXI DRIVER waits, exhales angrily.

Chris opens his wallet, puts it away, re-counts crumpled dollar bills and coins in his hand.

> CHRIS
> (ashamed)
> Look … I've got six bucks and
> some change.

> TAXI DRIVER
> Eight-fifty.

> CHRIS
> I just got out of jail. Here, take
> what I got and I'll send you the rest
> if you –

Driver grabs money.

> TAXI DRIVER
> Got a lighter?

> CHRIS
> Yeah. Sure.

> TAXI DRIVER
> Gimme.

Chris hands him a nice Zippo. Driver guns the engine and zooms away; Chris jumps back to avoid injury.

INT. BREMER LOBBY – DAY

SECURITY GUARD looks up, bored, behind a small shabby desk with a wilted rubber tree in a plain tiled lobby.

Chris enters, dejected, pastes a smile on his face again.

> CHRIS
> Hey, Jimmy, what's up?

Guard reaches in a pigeonhole, plops a handful of white and tan envelopes – Chris's mail – on the counter.

> SECURITY GUARD
> Got outta jail.

> CHRIS
> (shrugs)
> Yeah. Justifiable. Got yelled at. Still
> in business.

> SECURITY GUARD
> Treloar's gonna change the lock if you
> don't give him some dough. You're
> two months behind.

Chris opens letter, wilts.

> CHRIS
> Notice to quit or pay rent – which
> I can't right now. Can you talk to
> him for me? I just need a couple
> weeks to catch up.

Guard shakes his head, snorts.

> SECURITY GUARD
> Told me he's gonna cut my hours or
> pay, or both. Fired the janitor yesterday.
> While you were out.

CHRIS
(rubs his face)

Oh, man. Jim, I – I need a couple weeks.
I got receivables.

SECURITY GUARD

Want my advice?

CHRIS

Sure.

SECURITY GUARD

Move out before Treloar calls the
locksmith.

INT. OFFICE CORRIDOR

Chris exits elevator, walks briskly down corridor, turns corner, passes double glass doors with big letters: Treloar Investments.

He continues to walk, ice in his veins, passes many doors with cheap small plaques -- Bright Music, Daring Intl. Films, Prof. E. Hopgash, Tipper Home Loans, etc.

Near the end of the corridor there is a hardshell American Tourister suitcase directly in front of an office door.

Chris halts, cocks one eye at it.

He walks quietly, circling suitcase. It's directly in front of his office door: Cable Investigations.

Chris drops to his haunches, gazes under suitcase. He leans to the side and inspects the gap between door and suitcase. He puts a key in the door, opens it, carefully steps over the suitcase.

INT. CHRIS'S OFFICE – DAY

He gently closes office door, removes his jacket and hangs it on a coat rack, crosses office to a closet.

Chris dons a bulky bulletproof vest.

He moves to a battered file cabinet and pulls out toolcase, puts it quietly on his desk. Almost soundlessly sorts a selection of tools, finds a Dremel tool, tests the battery, sets it down, quietly and quickly unrolls other gear.

Chris unplugs his desk telephone, frowns, thinks briefly, goes back to file cabinet, gets white cotton gloves and fingerprint kit.

He empties a letter tray, puts selected tools and supplies in it, goes back to the closet, dons eye protection.

INT. OFFICE CORRIDOR

Chris quietly opens his office door, leaves it open. He returns with tray of tools and supplies, carefully steps over the suitcase, puts tray on floor.

He removes eye protection, takes loupe from tray, examines suitcase latches and exterior metal seams, puts loupe in pocket.

His white cotton gloves lightly touch the seams. Chris puts gloved fingers to his nose and sniffs.

He puts glasses back on, takes Dremel tool, positions it carefully, grimaces, and drills hole in top of suitcase.

The drill slams down loudly on thin metal suitcase. Beads of perspiration trickle down Chris's face. He drills another hole with greater care, puts down Dremel motor and wipes his brow.

NEARBY

Another office door opens and a slim, attractive woman (PEACHY) in skirt and high heels appears. She cocks her head, puzzled at scene of Chris, tools, suitcase.

CHRIS

Go away. Go back inside.

She frowns at him, closes and locks her office door (labelled "Mary Blount, CPA") then stands quietly in corridor sizing him up.

Chris inserts a fiber optic light into one drilled hole, positions battery on floor, clicks slide switch. High heels tap the floor, appearing at his side.

CHRIS

Quiet! Take your shoes off.

She raises an eyebrow, amused, sits on her haunches next to Chris, watches him.

PEACHY

Did you lose the key?

Chris inserts another fiber optic line with an eyepiece.

CHRIS

It's not mine. And it might be a
bomb, Peachy. So, take off those
extremely cute shoes – quietly!
Carry them in your hand and walk
to the nearest fire extinguisher in
case this doesn't turn out very
nicely.

PEACHY
My name isn't "Peachy"... it's
Mary.

Chris twists the fiber line, examining inside of suitcase.

CHRIS
Go away. (beat) I can't see much of
anything with this scope...

(stern)
And I don't have any money and
Treloar's going to kick me out, so
you're wasting you're time. Beat it.

Peachy studies him, glances at "Cable Investigations" sign on door,
frowns at Chris. He pulls fiber optic lines out of the suitcase.

PEACHY
I think it's just a suitcase. Left
here by mistake. Is there a label
on it or a monogram?

Chris carefully ties a loop of twine through the handle.

CHRIS
Open your office door. Hurry.

Chris unravels twine, walks to Peachy's office door. She follows,
unlocks and opens the door. Both step inside. He shoves her to the
wall, away from the open door.

CHRIS
Duck and cover, Peachy.

Chris yanks on twine.

Suitcase falls on tile floor, sounds empty.

Peachy covers her mouth, tries to suppress laughter.

Chris exhales, wipes brow, struggles out of body armor, smiles good-natured at Peachy.

> CHRIS
> Okay. You were right. It's a suitcase.

INT. CHRIS' OFFICE – DAY

Peachy watches Chris dust the suitcase for fingerprints.

> PEACHY
> Why did you think it was a bomb?

> CHRIS
> Why are you still here?

Peachy smiles.

> PEACHY
> I think you're an interesting person --
> even if you're as broke as you say you
> are. Who does your taxes?

> CHRIS
> I don't pay taxes.

He slowly lifts a thumbprint on wide clear tape.

ROB ~

What is this?

ALAN ~

I'm writing a screenplay out of sequence. I previously posted Sc. 36 *[at the B-List office]* Care to propose which scene I should write next?

1 2 3   7 8 9 10 11 12 13 14 15 16 17 18 19 20 21 22

23 24 25 26 27 28 29 30 31 32 33 34 35 37 38 39 40

ROB ~

Write the one that gets you most excited, I'd say.

ALAN ~

Yes, that makes sense, but I like all of them equally and they're all equally difficult.

More importantly, I'm demonstrating that each scene should be conceived and written as a mini-movie (beginning-middle-end) that has to stand on its own with one unrepeated dramatic action verb or keyword per scene, using Scene Card logic.

The sequence above was written against these 3x5 cards --

04. BEGS - gets out of taxi, old office bldg, guy at front desk, collects mail

05. COLD - suitcase in front of office, gets Dremel + fiber optic, gloves

06. HOT - sniffs, drills, Peachy the CPA is curious, suitcase is empty

The other reason to write out of sequence is to hone your skills. Many assignments as a pro screenwriter are to fix a scene or re-write a sequence. You don't get to rewrite the whole story, and have to hit certain "beats." Professional work is less about being excited and more about crafting to a brief.

That raises the question about spec scripts vs assignments. I wrote six or seven spec scripts (can't remember exactly), then I re-wrote and polished two of them and pitched Columbia, PSO, Al Ruddy, Kingman Films, DeLaurentiis and (can't remember exactly). Here's the bottom line. The *only* spec deal that got produced was a 12-page treatment that brought in the studio, two distribs, and the principal cast -- after which I co-wrote and doctored a shooting script. Most of the money I earned as a screenwriter was on assignment, usually uncredited.

I am not saying that spec scripts are unimportant. You can win with a spec script. But 9 times out of 10, it's a calling card. I turned down a lot of assignment work, holding out for my original stories and scripts. In retrospect, that was a mistake. It's easier to sell an original script *after* you've built a reputation fulfilling and completing writing assignments.

Since there haven't been any replies yet, I'll blather on about another issue, i.e., scene length. You can't tell a mini-story in 1/8 of a page. Yet a lot of newbies scatter-shoot incredibly short vignettes (sometimes single images!) that jump around to numerous locales and introduce dozens of named characters. Bill knows the "noir" script I'm thinking of in particular, but I've seen lots of other people do the same thing.

My advice: Stay in one place for two or three pages with a reasonably small number of named characters. Your main character should be on screen in almost every scene. Budget 40 scenes, not 60 or 100, and try to re-use some locations (INT. OFFICE, INT. MANSION) so it's relatively easy and inexpensive to shoot. Smart producers want to spend money on talent rather than transport and travel time, and splurge on one or two big stunt/action sequences instead of ten.

Simplify. Give your stars some meaty dialogue to chew on. Think legitimate (stage play) theater. Ham it up.

One of the main criticisms of my writing style is that I'm "too visual." Actually found a handwritten sticky note in one of my scripts saying "too visual" -- apparently an F with one of the development execs that I pitched, the same broad who counselled me to watch three movies a week and try to write something like KARATE KID or ROCKY.

It's true. I write a lot of visual continuity (action descriptions) and I'm inclined to tell stories in pictures. That's why I make a special effort to write four- or five- page dialogue scenes, too.

Hey, that's what I'll do next in my Writing Roulette game: the big dialogue scene where Chris confronts Spurls at his mansion, Sc. 18.

BILL ~

I'm reading (and watching) this script unfold with great interest, Alan, and look forward to its completion. I understood your scene card logic when you initially posted it here but I couldn't get your method to work for me. However, seeing it now being applied I understand the method better and will try it again. One thing needs clarification though - at least for dumbos like me! You have started off each post by stating the page numbers in the script that these scenes will appear in, but how have you decided that at this stage of the writing?

ALAN ~

The short answer, Bill, is long experience with movie budgeting. Any project of any length must be converted to shooting days, cast, crew, equipment, vehicles, staff, services, supplies, post production, laboratory, production insurance, publicity. Let's suppose I don't have an infinite budget and can't afford to dawdle forever, primarily because cast and crew will get bored. Same thing with audiences. They get bored. So it makes sense (to me) to budget how many pages each scene should be and what it should achieve. I'm not perfect. Some scenes are shorter than I budgeted, some slightly longer. But targets are helpful.

Within each scene, I have to do A, B, C, and budget space accordingly. There's plenty of room for creativity within an outline or budget. Sometimes I miss the mark.

Another formative experience was film editing, traditionally called cutting, literally with scissors in the old days. Two feet, seven feet, a few inches -- but never single frames. Physically handling film gave me a deeper appreciation of time, timing, shot sequences. The German filmmaker G.W. Pabst spoke of building a scene "brick-by-brick," compared to Sergei Eisenstein's theory of contradiction. Both are valid, but none more than D.W. Griffith's achievement of smooth continuity, which we take for granted in watching multi-camera "live-switch" TV (multiple angles covering one place/time).

The central issue for a director is: How shall we cover this? For a production manager: What is it going to require to do this? Shooting out-of-sequence is the most economical way to make a movie. To do that, a director has to know how the dramatic goal of A will join with B, despite the fact that Scene A was shot days or weeks later than Scene B. Most people like to start (shooting or writing) with the opening sequence. I'm indifferent to it, and there are many examples in film history of shooting the crisis/confrontation first.

BILL ~

Thanks for the lengthy reply, Alan, though apologies for my question being so poorly worded that it led to that, so I'll try again if I may.

I understand that scenes are shot out of order, and why. I can also comprehend why (and how) you can write them out of order. What I fail to understand is how you can write them in random order whilst still apparently knowing at this stage what page number these scenes will appear on in the finished script.

For example, when you posted scene 36 you had a heading implying that this would be pages 74-78 in the finished script (which also implies that you had a total page length in mind), and when you posted scene 5 the heading implied this would be on pages 7-12 of the finished script. Are these page numbers definitive or are they mere approximations for now and may change as and when more scenes are written?

Of course maybe I should stop asking foolish questions. There is a saying here: *Children and fools shouldn't see a job half done* (i.e., because both types ask lots of foolish questions that would be answered and obvious if only they'd wait to see the finished work).

ROB ~

I do find this interesting. I think after all the scenes are written one needs to look at continuity though.

ALAN ~

I suppose you're right, Rob. I'm sort of indifferent to good stories and screenplays, although I think you and many other of our colleagues are gifted writers. I don't remember inviting anyone to join The B List because they were unqualified. So, this is a conversation among peers.

Style is a very personal thing. My methods aren't the best or only way to shape a project. And it has to do with my basic ambivalence about "good" work. In the beginning, I was in love with storytelling, especially my own stories. I passionately loved every foot of film I shot. Sometimes I cried on the set, it was so wonderful. I played and replayed films and videos I made, read and re-read stories and scripts I wrote. I still do. GOVERNOR MIKE made me cry last week.

But a clear head and open heart see power and virtue in the works of others, even in rough draft. It gives me great pleasure to find a new candidate to join our vagabond party. Sadly, they're hard to find.

Mustard! a round of Bacardi and Coke for those present!

I toast each and every one who loves the work of life and love.

– p.s. about continuity, anything cuts with anything.

Bill, in The Golden Age of Hollywood, when staff screenwriters were assigned in groups and yanked off a project and replaced, scripts underwent a lot of revisions by multiple typewriters. A first draft was white, revised pages were canary, blue, pink, green (if I remember the order correctly) and inserted in 3-ring binders on the set when new or replacement pages arrived, often unexpectedly.

So, page numbers are just temporary. There may be some #__(a) or #__ blanks inserted.

Something similar happens when we improvise on the set, or in film editing. Big difference between an original screenplay, a shooting script, and final continuity (as shot and edited) that's used for ADR and "labial adaptation" used for foreign language dubbing.

BILL ~

Thank you, Mustard. I just love a Bacardi and Coke -- especially with a slice of lime and lots of ice. Thank you also Alan for allowing me to observe your working practices and learn from them.

;-)

Aaron Sorkin
Follows Alan's Advice

JIM ~

There are index cards everywhere in Aaron Sorkin's office. Index cards for scenes from films going back to 2007's Charlie Wilson's War.

The writer of The West Wing and The Social Network likes to use those cards, tacked to a large corkboard, to keep track of key elements. Social Network's pivotal scenes are still up there, with notes that read, "Mark and Erica in bar," "Mark walks back to dormitory" and "Mark begins drinking, blogging, hacking."

[Hollywood Reporter, 1/8/11]

ALAN ~

Hey, cut that out. (laughs)

ROB ~

Saw him on the Today Show, this AM. Great guy.

I've used the cards. I even took to using 5X8 (size up from 3X5) for the slugs to scenes and use a felt marker so I can see it from a distance. 3X5s became shots (paragraphs) down the page. I'd love to roll in front of ACT I (and the rest) in my office chair and browse through the movie.

Too many people make the whole show up as they go along, and, that's alright, maybe, to an extent if they're seasoned enuf to be certain where they're going. You know that song. "Goin' ta Kansas City, Kansas City here I come... I might take a train, might take a plane, but if I hafta' walk, I'll get there the same." Well, Kansas City is the climax and it shouldn't ever happen by accident.

Staring, mezmerized at a couple cork boards for a while, rolling the film, gets a writer real objective to the story. Becoming interiorized into a story can cause one to become lost and writer's block. It's like standing under an elephant and only seeing gray.

Great article Jim. Thanks.

JIM ~

Come on, Alan. Admit it. You taught the man everything he knows! But seriously, there is the 'great minds think alike' factor in play here.

Sorkin does a lot of what I do, only in the big time. Besides his more public successes, he gets paid a small fortune for doing uncredited rewrite/polish work.

ALAN ~

I learned Scene Card technique (using one action word) from the late Alejandro Rey, a terrific mentor who also showed me how to direct actors. Not knowing how else to thank a dead guy for launching my career, I'll reprint a little tribute I wrote a long time ago.

It wasn't hard to find Alejandro's house. Sunset to Vista, turn right, half a block, private cul-de-sac. Two story villa on the left. Like most of the homes in the Hollywood Hills, a blue octagonal sign on the lawn warned potential intruders that armed guards were on the prowl, whenever they were needed.

Whitney rang the bell with a slumped shoulder and a sagging spirit. He might as well be calling on his own executioner. After a lengthy wait, he rang again.

The director greeted him with a look of confusion, then recognition.

"Ah, Robert!" he remembered, " —please come in. Please. How are you today?"

A maid received sharp instructions in Spanish, which was Alejandro's native tongue. Whitney glanced at the gracefully off white interior filled with beautiful furniture, deep-pile carpets, sensually clean metal and glass, delicate sculpture and precious object d'art. "Come—come," Alejandro beckoned with the rich, rolling accent of an elegant Latin tradition.

The garden patio breathed cool green relief, in the shade of fragrant eucalyptus and soft fallen leaves. A sweeping symphony rolled through the patio from hidden speakers. Alejandro graciously ordered wine glasses and a snack, delighted to receive his young guest with hospitality. With the slightest possible suggestion of disapproval, he provided an ashtray for Whitney's cigarette. Alejandro preferred to smoke a freshly rolled marijuana joint, and smiled gaily as he lit it.

There were a few introductory questions—some pertaining to Larry, which Whitney failed to answer; many pertaining to Whitney himself and the story he had co-authored. "Oh, yes," Alejandro stated with deep sincerity, " —it is a marvelous story. Very strong. Very nice. And those pages you have finished of the script— wonderful!—the first scene is excellent!"

Whitney felt himself opening to this man. He was thin, like Whitney. He was alert and intelligent. He was the same height. But something more—something more than just a physical resemblance was grow- ing between them. It was the uncanny feeling of familiarity, as if he was speaking to himself—to the self he had known years ago, long before he came to Hollywood.

Alejandro was respectful and deferential, although he clearly didn't have to be. "Would you feel more comfortable working on the script by yourself?" he asked Whitney, "—or would you consider working with me to help you?" The straightforward innocence in Alejandro's voice convinced him to say 'yes,' he would like to have his help.

On his next visit to Alejandro's house, Whitney found the front door ajar and a pretty girl on the living room sofa, anxiously fingering the pages of a script. She looked up and they exchanged hellos. Presently, a big, nervous young man tromped up the flagstone steps and joined them. Alejandro's voice could be heard from another room. The boy and girl commiserated with desperate but guarded worry. They were going to debut in a new play – one of Hollywood's endless showcases for new playwrights and aspiring actors.

When Alejandro entered the room, he greeted Whitney and apologized—Would he allow him to coach these two actors for a few minutes, as a favor to a friend? Whitney was amazed by the director's courtesy and consideration. "Of course," he mumbled with embarrassment.

"You are very kind, Robert. Would you like to watch? It's good to have an audience."

Alejandro had never met these kids before in his life. He knew nothing about them or their script. And yet he knew everything.

"Read your lines," he instructed them, "and read them exactly as you will perform them on your opening night."

"B-but... you mean, just cold, right now?"

"Yes, of course. There is never a rehearsal on stage—only a performance. Give me everything you can."

They plodded and heaved through a few meaningless lines of dialogue.

"Go back to the beginning of the scene," Alejandro abruptly directed. The nervous lad fumbled, and then uttered the first few words of his speech again.

"What do you mean?" Alejandro interrupted.

"I'm sorry—" the boy said, stunned.

"You said: 'This wayward soul, this place we call our future...' and whatever else was next," Alejandro insisted. "What do you mean?"

The boy was more confused. "You mean what do the words mean?"

"No, no!—you, the character. What do you mean when you say those words?"

The boy feverishly scanned his script.

"It's not in your script," the director said, shaking his head solemnly. "Forget the words—they can be any words. If they are words written by a playwright in Hollywood, they are probably stupid words to begin with. But what do you mean at this moment? What do you feel in your heart? In your guts. In your cock."

The boy swallowed and took the plunge. "Well," he mumbled, "I think it's fear, maybe."

"Good. Now say the words."
"This wayward soul..."

"What do you mean?"

"I'm sorry, I don't understand," the boy helplessly confessed.

"Here," Alejandro commanded. "I am going to ask you questions, and you answer me, but say the words in the script—understand? Answer me any way you can, but you must use the words of your speech. Yes?"

"Alright."

"NO !—Answer me with the words of your speech. Do you understand?"

A look of comprehension spread slowly over the boy's face. He nodded carefully.

"Say the words."

The boy blinked and mumbled "This wayward soul" in a tone that indicated his willingness to go on.

"Good. Now, did you come here for help?"

Catching on, the boy finished the line, conveying his gratitude: "—this place we call a future!"

"What do you think of this play?"

The boy's eyes widened, and then he charged into the next two lines of his speech, clearly conveying his disdain for all the symbolic rubbish that filled this play and made the dopey dialogue incredibly hard to memorize.

"Excellent!" Alejandro decided. "Now, whenever I ask you 'What do you mean?' I want you to speak the words in this play, because that is what actors do. We say the words someone else has written. But now, let me see how you prepare..."

He guided the boy and girl through their scripts, asking them — not telling them — what each scene was about, what key lines of dialogue meant to their characters, how they felt at each point in the dialogue. Occasionally, they tried to ask the director for his advice or help. "No questions, please," he said sternly. "I ask the questions—not you." When it was finally established what each actor intended to portray at various passages, Alejandro called for another performance. "Remember, no rehearsals! This is the only performance you will ever give. So make it your best."

The two kids were much better, but Alejandro stopped them from time to time, asking What do you mean? and What do your hands mean? and What do your legs mean? until both actors were expressing their inner motivation through each and every part of their bodies.

"Come here," he instructed the girl, taking her aside. He whispered a long series of instructions to her. She nodded her agreement and they returned. "From the top!" he ordered—and suddenly the girl's performance came to life with ferocity, tenderness, delicacy and rage. Then the boy was brought within earshot of Whitney, while Alejandro whispered his special instructions to him: "When you say 'I will never leave you, I love you', I want you to imagine that you have an irresistible impulse to kick her very hard with your right leg. You don't do it, but you feel every muscle trying to achieve that impulse—do you understand? You must kick her, very hard when you say 'I will never leave you'—do you understand?"

As Whitney gaped in astonishment, the duo performed the scene again—and this time it was as vivid and as moving as any piece of professional drama ever staged by anyone on the planet.

Brandishing a limitless array of directorial weapons, Alejandro Vargas had transformed two utterly lousy novices into powerful actors, and he had done it in precisely seven minutes flat.

"Goodbye, goodbye—yes, thank you—good luck," he said to them as they left, then he turned to Whitney and apologized again for the delay.

It was the first of many lessons to come.

JIM ~

Wow!

ALAN ~

I met Alejandro for the first time 30 years ago, got to work with him almost every day for a month. I was writing an action movie; he was signed to direct. Before the deal blew up, I learned a hell of a lot from him. Dissatisfied with the idea that I was living in a cheap motel room on Melrose, he put me into a fully furnished penthouse in a nice apartment building he owned that was across the cul de sac from his house. When I got stuck for an idea or got tired of sitting at the typewriter, the patio overlooked Sunset Boulevard, the Playboy Building, Le Dome, Puck's.

Alejandro had interesting friends. Outrageously beautiful women. Stacey Keach for a backgammon partner. Rode with him in his ancient Mercedes on occasion, I forget where exactly – downtown Hollywood, Bel Air, Beverly Hills. His wife and son lived next door to Richard Dawson.

Years later I came back to Hollywood, and Alejandro hadn't changed. Still brilliant and handsome and blackballed by the studios, because he did The Flying Nun series with Sally Field and because every movie they cast him in after that, Alejandro diplomatically tried to save the poor boob who was sitting in the director's chair. He was pals with Sarandon, Franciosa. Coached everybody.

When I got fed up with Hollywood (again) and went to live on a ranch in North California, I kept in touch with him by phone. Said he was bitten by an insect out in the Mojave on location for an A-Team episode, playing the bad guy of course. A couple weeks later, BBC World Service said Alejandro had died of lung cancer. I called Ned Mandarino, a close friend and colleague of Alejandro's who wrote a very important textbook called *The Transpersonal Actor*. Ned told me when the memorial was scheduled. I flew down on a puddle jumper and an indie distributor friend drove me to the cemetery.

No fan club, no press. Just me and 100 stars and a handful of young proteges who came to weep. I still visit his grave whenever I'm in town, although I'm no longer active in show business.

This long-winded spiel is about mentors. I was very lucky indeed. Charlie Sciurba, A.S.C., taught me cinematography in Milwaukee when I was a teenager. Alejandro Rey, D.G.A., taught me the craft of organizing a story and the art of directing. I had to learn editing the hard way, by doing it, in a lot of different film guages and video formats and mixing rooms in L.A., Amsterdam, Sydney, London.

It's no secret that my "career" never really took off. I made some shows I'm proud of. My first feature was a legal and financial disaster, never released. And I retired from show business about the time Wolf DeVoon disappeared from Zoetrope in 2005. A small stroke knocked out my creative power.

Those who can, do. Those who can't, tell war stories and offer little homilies about Scene Cards and the evils of flashbacks.

Q. When you were brought in to doctor THE GODFATHER script, were you given certain sections or the entire screenplay?

I was given certain sections. The main problem was that there was no final scene between Michael Corleone and his father. Since he was about 4 or 5 weeks into shooting, Francis Coppola didn't know what to do about it. He kept saying, "I want a scene where they say they love each other." I couldn't write a scene with two people saying they love each other. It had to be about something, an action. So that scene in the garden between Al Pacino and Marlon Brando is what I ended up doing -- a scene about the transfer of power.

(Robert Towne)

I told Rossen he ought to somehow liken what Eddie does [in THE HUSTLER] to what anybody who's performing something sensational is doing -- a ball player, say, or some guy who laid 477 bricks in one day. Well, we were shooting on 55th Street in New York, and Bob listened to what I said, and we walked into his office, and it couldn't have been 6 minutes later that he came out with the 4-page scene that was in the film.

(Paul Newman)

I had made up my mind not to be bound by the script [PANIC IN THE STREETS, 1950]. It is the first time I threw the script over. We had a property truck with a typewriter on the back of it, on the tailgate. Every morning the writer [Richard Murphy] came to work with me... we would redo every scene...

(Elia Kazan)

Story
Development

Theme
Plot
Character
Style

FFC on theme

SALLY (quoting Francis Ford Coppola) ~

When you make a movie, always try to discover what the theme of the movie is in one or two words. Every time I made a film, I always knew what I thought the theme was, the core, in one word. In "The Godfather," it was succession. In "The Conversation," it was privacy. In "Apocalypse," it was morality.

The reason it's important to have this is because most of the time what a director really does is make decisions. All day long: Do you want it to be long hair or short hair? Do you want a dress or pants? Do you want a beard or no beard? There are many times when you don't know the answer. Knowing what the theme is always helps.

I remember in "The Conversation," they brought all these coats to me, and they said: Do you want him to look like a detective, Humphrey Bogart? Do you want him to look like a blah blah blah. I didn't know, and said the theme is 'privacy' and chose the plastic coat you could see through. So knowing the theme helps you make a decision when you're not sure which way to go.

-- Francis Ford Coppola in *The 99 Percent*

TOM ~

Thanks for posting this, Sally. There is a problem with having a one word theme -- it doesn't capture the real theme. Themes make a statement on an issue. All the choices a filmmaker makes is a statement of belief. Everything we see from a filmmaker is that person's take on the issue at hand. However, the nice thing about a single word theme is that it forces you to focus. Focus on what you are trying to say.

Theme, Plot, Characterization

ALAN ~

It may be entirely synthetic -- a fantasy -- or clothed in highly recognizable time and place. It could be terrifying, gentle, peculiar, or plain. But all stories have certain elements that are inherent to the fine art of literature, as I understand it.

Theme

Creation of a story begins with an idea, something that inspires the writer to invest time and diligent effort, to the exclusion of other pursuits. The idea must be compelling to its author, or it won't get written. We often see a character and a situation first, a tangible subject for a story. But stories do not write themselves. The author brings perspective and passion to the subject, and with it, the power to transform a flash into a fully formed commitment. I will tell the story of honor, of life on life's terms, of youthful adventure, of crime's dark and dingy impoverishment, of gaeity, of devotion and skill. Such abstract concepts are thematic. Whether you consciously choose a theme or not, if you have any love of storytelling, your work always proceeds thematically. It shapes your selection of characters, the events of a plot, and the crucial moment you love best in the writing, when the theme stands clear and proud, because **this** is what I am trying to say. (Hugo's *Notre Dame de Paris* = fatality)

Plot

A story in which nothing happens is not a story. Personally, I don't think plot is half as important as theme. The plot of BEING THERE (1979 directed by Hal Ashby, adapted from the 1971 novella by Jerzy Kosinski) is thin and improbable. But it has a compelling theme: that *simplicity is no different than genius.* Whether you agree with me about this deconstruction is less important than seeing the difference between theme and plot. A plot may be spectacular, urgent, and tense. It may be leisurely at first and then suddenly desperate and dark. Selection of plot structure and pace, in my view, should be a means to an end -- that is: tailored to explicate and explore a great theme.

Good stories address something bigger, exploring The Unknown, no roadmap to success. Joseph Campbell's hero's journey takes the hero underground. Sometimes survival of an adventure is enough to constitute moral victory.

Characterization

I'm not a big fan of historical literature or archtypal heroes, villians, damsels in distress, or stock characters that we've seen a million times (a cop, a waitress, an old man). It would be better not to have characters at all, unless they are new and original people that rivet our attention, both as writer and reader, because we have not seen them before. I know that's asking a lot. Writers are in competition with approximately 1000 great authors in good libraries and 1 million crummy ones. I urge you to stop reading other authors. There is nothing to be gained in character development by "borrowing." I love Raymond Chandler to bits, but could not (honestly incapable of it) transplant Philip Marlowe into one of my stories, without reneging the joy of writing my theme, my plot, and my cast of characters.

Style

I often say, style is a very personal thing. It would be foolish to categorize five or six examples of style and suggest you pick one like ready-to-wear pants. Archaic popular writers like Twain and O Henry are a pain to read compared to Fitzgerald, for instance. Straight, simple and deep may be too much to ask of myself or anyone else. Talent is honed by experience, but I think great writers are born, not made.

It doesn't trouble me to be a second-class writer. The style I developed is my own and it came naturally, organically, although I had to learn a few lessons the hard way. I still use too many commas. In writing this little paragraph it was necessary to go back and delete ten of them. If this paragraph had been written for a story I would have edited it a thousand times, cutting repetitive words and listening to the metre of each phrase. I hammer out big chunks in first draft, then craft my work with a needle. It takes hours and days and months to do a good job, and the result is my own voice, because no one else loved it and labored over it.

Target audience

Pick a sympathetic main character with something unusual; special abilities (super sharp hearing, super smart) or handicap (recently defeated, lonesome) or both. A main character the target group will identify with and find likeable.

Love interest

Approximately the same age, a natural antagonist, but secretly bonded to the main character and ready to help.

Maguffin

A thing, natural phenomenon, or problem that defies explanation. Establish early.

Raymond Chandler kept a chapbook, notes to himself, that were published after his death as addenda to the 2nd volume of a library edition of his collected works. Great advice about storytelling:

1. "It must be credibly motivated, both as to original situation and the denouement; it must consist of plausible actions of plausible people

in plausible circumstances, it being remembered that plausibility is largely a matter of style. This requirement rules out most trick endings...

2. "It must be technically sound. No snakes climbing up bellropes ("The Speckled Band"). Such things at once destroy the foundation of the story...

3. "It must be honest with the reader. This is always said, but the implications are not realized. Important facts must not only must not be concealed, they must not be distorted by false emphasis. Unimportant facts must not be projected in such a way as to make them portentous...

4. "It must be realistic as to character, setting, and atmosphere. It must be about real people in a real world...

5. "It must have a sound story value...

6. "To achieve this it must have some form of suspense, even if only intellectual. This does not mean menace...

7. "It must have color, lift, and a reasonable amount of dash. It takes an awful lot of technical adroitness to compensate for a dull style, although it has been done, especially in England.

8. "It must have enough essential simplicity to be explained when the time comes (This is possibly the most often violated of all the rules.) The ideal denouement is one in which everything is revealed in a flash of action. This is rare because ideas that good are rare...

9. "It must baffle a reasonably intelligent reader...

10. "The solution must seem inevitable once revealed. This is the least often emphasized element of a good mystery, but it is one of the important elements of all fiction...

11. "It must not try to do everything at once. If it is a puzzle story operating in a rather cool, reasonable atmosphere, it cannot be a vio-

lent adventure or a passionate romance. An atmosphere of terror destroys logical thinking; if the story is about the intricate psychological pressures that lead apparently ordinary people to commit murder, it cannot then switch to the cool analysis of the police investigator. The detective cannot be hero and menace at the same time; the murderer cannot be a tortured victim of circumstance and also a heavy.

12. "It must punish the criminal in one way or another, not necessarily by operation of law..."

Of course, Chandler was talking about murder mysteries, his stock in trade, but I believe those 12 rules apply to all stories and 90-minute screenplays in particular.

A generation gap

ALAN ~

Discussion on the Main board about Kubrick's BARRY LYNDON got me thinking about our difference in ages, cultures, and traditions. Not to criticize or complain. I merely want to make a few notes about cinema.

Sergei Eisenstein, BATTLESHIP POTEMKIN
… pioneer of montage and sequence of shots

G.W. Pabst, THE JOYLESS STREET
… pioneer of intimate direct continuity

F.W. Murnau, THE LAST LAUGH, SUNRISE
… pioneer of moving camera

Alfred Hitchcock, THE PARADINE CASE, FRENZY
… pioneer of the match dissolve

Carol Reed, ODD MAN OUT, FALLEN IDOL, THE THIRD MAN
… master of moody noir

John Ford, THE INFORMER, STAGECOACH, THE GRAPES OF WRATH, FORT APACHE, THE SEARCHERS
… pioneer of location shoot, panoramic long shot

Jean Renoir, GRAND ILLUSION, THE RULES OF THE GAME
"the greatest of all directors" (Orson Welles)

George Stevens, THE DIARY OF ANNE FRANK, A PLACE IN THE SUN, SHANE, GIANT … master of intimate drama

Frank Capra, MEET JOHN DOE, IT'S A WONDERFUL LIFE, MR SMITH GOES TO WASHINGTON
… uniquely passionate and creative American storyteller

William Wyler, WUTHERING HEIGHTS, MRS MINIVER, ROMAN HOLIDAY, FUNNY GIRL
… uniquely gifted "actor's director"

Akiro Kurosawa, RASHOMON, SEVEN SAMURAI, YOJIMBO
… master of ensemble cast and graphic violence

Stanley Kubrick, DR STRANGELOVE, 2001, CLOCKWORK ORANGE, THE SHINING
… incomparable innovator of cinematic techniques

Fred Zinneman, HIGH NOON, FROM HERE TO ETERNITY, DAY OF THE JACKAL
… master of realism, realistic pace and authenticity

Robert Stevenson, OLD YELLER, KIDNAPPED, MARY POPPINS
… king of Disney family entertainment

Blake Edwards, PETER GUNN (TV), OPERATION PETTICOAT, PINK PANTHER SERIES
… meticulous king of farce

John Huston, THE MALTESE FALCON, KEY LARGO, THE AFRICAN QUEEN, THE MISFITS
… superbly confident writer-director

Bob Fosse, CABARET, ALL THAT JAZZ
… master of filmed choreography

When we write for the screen, consider how much was defined and achieved by our predecessors. If you haven't seen most of the movies mentioned above, your education is incomplete.

Sorry to nag, but that's what I'm here for.

DAVID ~

I think I would respectfully question this assumption.

If one wants to create a modern romance then elements of the classics may be useful, but elements of modern classics may be as important if not more so. They may be able to draw on modern and classic romances and certainly there may be value in seeing other classics as may apply to their particular industry...

For my own studies of film, I have explored films from other countries and cultures nearly as much as I have studied films made in this country. To me it seems that with international markets for films and increasing exposure in this culture to international films, these are just as relevant in forming my ideas...

However, I find that older films seem less inspiring and nourishing than modern. I pay attention to elements that are classic and consistent then and now and figure that is part of what makes things universal and timeless...

My interest as a screenwriter is to innovate not to duplicate...

I personally prefer to identify my personal classics and perhaps shows that are classic among certain groups of people to explore and reference... a Bollywood classic, a Scorcese piece on Tibet, a Hitchcock without demanding I see every Hitchcock, a classic teen movie like AMERICAN PIE...

I do appreciate the posting of this list and enjoyed seeing that I had seen a number of them. Probably not half and I may consider seeking out certain ones. so thank you for posting and while we obviously do not agree entirely on this subject, the value of studying classics in some form I think is clearly there.

ALAN ~

That's an excellent reply David, really just what I was hoping for, a dialogue. I'm unable to talk about modern films or modern literature, being a dinosaur and a rather ignorant one (aren't all dinosaurs?)

Please talk about modern works.

TONY ~

What an amazing post and reply.

I've seen most of films listed just in the course of going to the movies my entire life. Never consciously studied any of them but I think you tend to remember what you like. I like the old classics although they might not be contemporary, they reflect a time and place and a certain humanity I find lacking in a lot of modern fare particulary TV. Of course there are many exceptions, but overall I think a lot of what we see today is contrived.

I also believe movies are the literature of modern times and as such there is a certain responsibility to enhance the human experience rather than just titillate. People should take away some understanding of life. Tough to do when your target audience is 15 year old boys.

One of these responsibilities is to pass down knowledge, or teach if you will. Culture is knowledge. Thanks guys for an amazing post.

RLB ~

Define modern.

Off the top of my head, the films I remember admiring are things like Gone With the Wind, High Noon, Stagecoach, a few Clint Eastwood spaghetti westerns (mainly for the theme music), Wuthering Heights, Rebecca, The Birds, and Lord of the Rings. Most of the Narnia series and early M. Night Shaymalan (I could look up the spelling but am too lazy). Not much before 1950, not much after 1980. Leaves a pretty small window... I must be leaving out a number that I liked at the time or learned something from, but none springs to mind.

EDIT: Ah, yes, the post about Driving Miss Daisy reminded me of at least one more that ranks high on my list of favorites: To Kill A Mockingbird.

NAOMI ~

Thanks, Alan. There's a fair few here I'll add to my list. :)

But I gotta disagree again, that the reason I didn't get on with Barry Lyndon could be a generation gap. I have watched and enjoyed many films from all generations. I get the feeling I'm being labelled, at least a little, as some closed-minded action blockbuster junkie with no attention span -- and that's SO far from the truth!

ALAN ~

My supposition about "a generation gap" was based on personal experience. When 2001 A SPACE ODYSSEY was first released, I was a teenager and it shattered me, really forged within me the desire to pursue a career in filmmaking. Unforgettable. Then I saw it again in 1990 at the Tuschinsky in Amsterdam. Kubrick's 2-D cutouts of the TWA shuttle and circular Space Station were appalling. The pace seemed horribly slow. I was a generation older.

Now here we are, you and I, discussing BARRY LYNDON, another museum piece. Personally I don't want to see it again, because Kubrick's shocking achievement of 1977, shooting candlelight with fast primes means nothing today. Fairly common set-up now.

Tell me about the pictures you like.

DAVID ~

As far as modern films, the film that for me made me want to write was The Matrix. To be fair, I was a 28 or 27 year old boy at the time, living in a large city. It was a doorway. I still like the film for a lot of reasons. It was very compelling visually, and it remains of course a modern classic for many people. You can see influences of it through-out the sci fi and spy genres in TV and film.

Now, there is the action side of things, but Matrix also has a philo-sophy to it and archetypal structuring that offers a resonance for a lot of people.

I don't have some agenda that everyone should like it. But for me it was one of the first films that said to me: Action and philosophy can mix. Kill Bill was gruesome in some ways, but added its own mix...

The Prestige was a film that stuck with me, and I got a copy of the screenplay. It has a dynamic between the two characters that is enga-ging and painful to watch. It cuts deep into the psyche and mirrors sometimes the way dynamics can be tormented throughout life for decades, if not the rest of one's life. There is an intimacy to the film which stood out to me. It was set in the past. but it felt timeless to me.

V for Vendetta spoke to a desire to deconstruct society that many have and feel. Fight Club mirrored that. I think they are definitely classics for many young men and guys up to the age of at least forty...

I am not a standard 'sci fi' lover as far as tech for the sake of tech, or cold visuals and sterile dialog that occurs in so many. But I am one for space dramas essentially and for the deeper philosophical elements which can be woven in with heart when done right.

People like cinematic explosions. People like action. They will watch a lot, if bookended with action or murder... A lot of the artistry comes in and around mayhem and how the mayhem is depicted.

Comedy

SALLY ~

Alan, I'm working my way through the older threads in this office (so much knowledge to glean). In a Nov 28 post, you wrote:

"Anything else you need to absorb is in classic films like THE MALTESE FALCON, MRS MINIVER, BRIDGE OVER THE RIVER KWAI, KHARTOUM, CLOCKWORK ORANGE, THE AFRICAN QUEEN, MEET JOHN DOE, MODERN TIMES, CHARLY, DOCTOR STRANGELOVE, BAMBI, BAD DAY AT BLACK ROCK, FRENZY, KEY LARGO."

I was wondering what you, or anyone else familiar with Golden Age films, would recommend for classic comedy films.

ALAN ~

I made a list of personal favorites

SAFETY LAST (1923)
THE GENERAL (1926)
CITY LIGHTS (1931)
MODERN TIMES (1936)
THE GREAT DICTATOR (1940)
HIS GIRL FRIDAY (1940)
TALK OF THE TOWN (1942)
ARSENIC AND OLD LACE (1944)
THE MOUSE THAT ROARED (1959)
DOCTOR STRANGELOVE (1964)
AFTER THE FOX (1966)
THE PRODUCERS (1968)
THE PINK PANTHER STRIKES AGAIN (1976)

also rans:

BRINGING UP BABY (1938)
SINGIN' IN THE RAIN (1952)
CALAMITY JANE (1953)
OPERATION PETTICOAT (1959)
THE ABSENT MINDED PROFESSOR (1961)

KEN ~

Duck Soup
The Fatal Glass of Beer

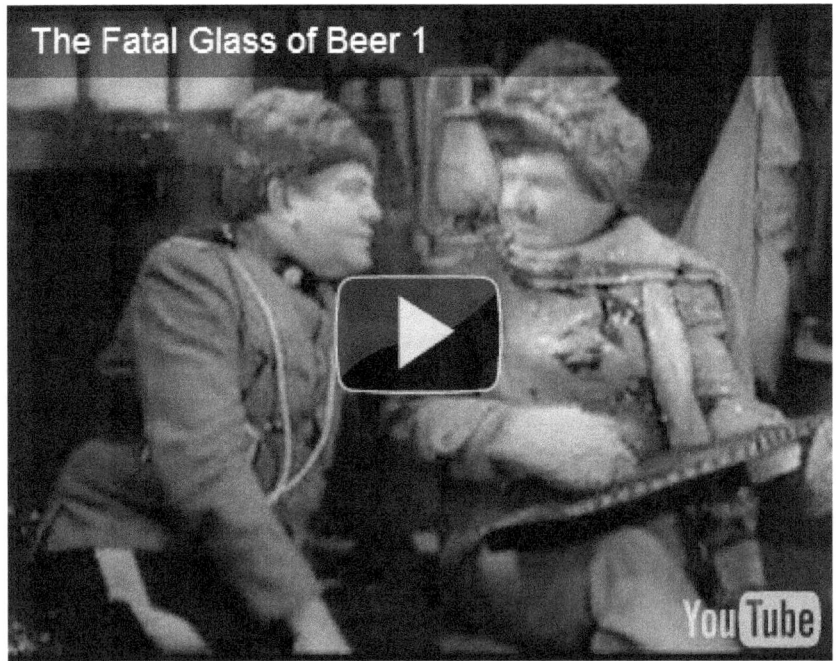

W.C. Fields (1933)

GREGOR ~

The Wrong Box or basically anything with Peter Sellers in it. He could walk by the set and make the film funnier.

FRANK ~

A Mad Mad Mad World

JOHN C. ~

A modern classic: Animal House

JULIE ANN ~

I love all of Jerry Lewis' movies, so be sure and put him on your list. Doris Day also did a ton of cute rom/coms.

SALLY ~

Thanks, Ken! - Duck Soup is at the top of my list, too.

Thank you everyone for your suggestions so far.

Now I'm curious: how many of these did you recommend as viewers because they are personal favourites, and how many of them did you recommend as writers because you think they are particularly well written?

JOHN C. ~

Comedy is personal. The movie Tootsie is touted in one book on movies as the "perfect comedy script." I found it funny at times, but uneven and overlong. Maybe seeing Dustin Hoffman in a dress was a turn-off.

If I had to limit myself to one favorite comedy, I'd pick The Apartment. It touches the heart, as well as the funny bone.

SALLY ~

Comedy is personal, but it's not arbitrary. No one is going to call Schindler's List a comedy. No one is going to call Duck Soup a tragedy.

In this room, I assume we all have a professional interest in film or in writing or both. (Am I wrong?) I'm really curious how many people here have the capacity to transcend their personal taste and talk, objectively, about the merits of a film. If "I like it" is one's only criteria, it's hard to have a professional conversation, and it's hard to communicate with other people and discuss things productively.

One of my favourite films is The Blues Brothers. I love it, and I can watch it repeatedly. But I don't think it is flawless (hardly), and I would never suggest it is a great or classic film.

Not everyone here writes comedy, or even thinks analytically about comedy. That's okay. But for those who can discuss comedy objectively, it's possible to have a meaningful discussion that isn't just a battle of subjective opinions.

Your comments in your post are great, and a great help, by example. I haven't seen Tootsie in dog's years, but the next time I see it, I will watch it for evenness and length. And I agree that in general, a lot of comedies suffer from unevenness.

JOHN C. ~

The Blues Brothers is also one of my favorite films. It's in the same category as Animal House, Blazing Saddles and Airplane: comic classics that withstand repeat viewings. That's because they are so densely packed with comic genius that they cannot be absorbed in one viewing. It's hard to appreciate them fully the first time around, especially when you are laughing too hard.

ROB ~

Being part of the Blues Brothers and Animal House production, I gotta say, it was the same party outside of film as in it. What a trip.

TONY ~

The Egg and I
Some Like It Hot
McClintock
Bachelor and the Bobby Soxer
At War With The Army
The Odd Couple

JONAS ~

Just lying in wait, ready to pounce on a subject at my level, like root beer consumption and Carry On flicks.

ERIK ~

Does anyone remember The Apple War (Swedish)? No copies any-where to be found nowadays.

GERRY ~

'The Man Who Would Be King' - better writing. And one of the best buddy movies, with an Englishman and a Scot!

John Wayne was in a great classic comedy. It's a rom-com with several twists. I've got you puzzled now, haven't I? Scroll down...

The Quiet Man.

SALLY ~

Haven't seen The Apple War or heard about it, Erik. Why has it stayed in your memory?

[to Gerry] ~ And Maureen O'Hara is fabulous in it, too.

GERRY ~

They are perfect opposites - it makes the whole film.

SALLY ~

Agreed. And the cross-country fight scene is one of my favourite scenes in film. It's up there with "I am Spartacus!" (which is hands-down my favourite scene).

ERIK ~

Exquisite rural setting to start; idyllic simple Swedish country folks; everyone knows everyone and gets along. Then the German land developers come to town in a huge Mercedes limo and talk up a huge Wally-World type of resort, planning to pave farmland and destroy waterfront. It looks like stereotype and that the little guys are powerless. Many of the stars of the Swedish cinema got involved; Max von Sydow plays a set of simpleton twins. Anyone who is still awake by this time gets to watch the community come together and begin to use their "abilities," previously undisclosed, to persuade the intruders to leave. Each has a different magic power which is used without injury, but makes the developers flee to keep their sanity. The war is between the gentle abilities of these folks and the mega-bucks and greed of the interlopers. It had a following in the U-District of Seattle when I was twenty or so. Saw it several times. Haven't seen hide nor hair in forty years. It does Google.

SALLY ~

It sounds fantastic, Erik. If you ever come across good source for it, let me know. I'd love to see it. And thank you for the summary.

JONAS [re 'The Quiet Man'] ~

Excellent film. I wish they had also made it earlier on with Spencer Tracy and Clark Gable as planned.

I've never been able to figure out why that movie don't do well at the box office. What more do you want from a film?

Minor characters

ALAN ~

Each scene should have a dramatic action, a purposeful engine expressed in one verb -- e.g., seek, struggle, surmount, see, question, doubt, deny, refuse, play, joke, evade, caress, surrender, ponder, decide, destroy, search, laugh, cry, carry on, tire, fall asleep, wake up – all of which are action verbs, something to do. Of necessity, one character has to carry the scene, because purposeful action is individual. I am opposed to ensemble dynamics, even when there is a team or romantic couple. In any given scene, one of them must lead and carry the action initially, and the progress and result of that scene consists in testing the leading action. It's always possible to be defeated or blunted by other characters, or by physical obstacles, or the lead's hubris or stupidity -- but each scene is *someone's* move on the chessboard.

Ray Chandler's "The Long Goodbye" is a good reference on what to do with a minor character who casts a long shadow. Billionaire Harlan Potter is always in the background. His daughter is in the first scene. Marlowe befriends a man who married her, divorced her, remarried her, and is accused of killing her. Throughout this 1st Act of a very long story, her billionaire father is constantly referenced. He sends an attorney to bail Marlowe out of jail. He suppresses the police investigation and silences newspapers. Another Potter daughter becomes involved in the 2nd act in multiple scenes, cautioning Marlowe not to cross her father's hush-up of what happened. **She takes Marlowe to meet him (one short scene).** The Potter wealth and influence continues to color the story to the very end, when Marlowe has a romantic encounter with the surviving Potter daughter.

Bottom line: give your minor character one scene, which he leads.

The What if ...? Game

JIM ~

Have you ever played the "what if..." game for coming up with story ideas?

I'll start...

What if, unbeknownst to him, a hit man's next assignment was an unkillable vampire?

Maybe we should make him a werewolf?

ROB ~

Goes to show, I'm not into horror. Werewolf is good, but no one knows that until act III. Maybe the hit man tracks the guy by the trail of savage killings. Maybe the hit man shoots him and it doesn't even phase the werewolf, until he gets him with a 50-cal. solid silver slug.

ALAN ~

Not hit man, unless it's a farce. Cop on the trail of serial killer vampire who can't be killed with lead. No place to get 50-cal silver, has to learn how to reload (see mausersandmuffins.blogspot.com). All his brother cops think he's lost his marbles.

ROB ~

I like that, Alan. He's gotta become obsessive on getting the guy. It's no surprise he loses his wife and family over it.

JIM ~

Maybe they think he's so nuts that they kick him off the force and he continues after the vampire as a civilian.

ROB ~

Yes! Then the police are against him and no one believes him, until the end!

JIM ~

Or perhaps it turns out he really is stark raving mad.

ALAN ~

How about two endings (insane, or succeeds in killing vampire). Either have audience vote on which final reel to exhibit -- digital projection makes this feasible -- or play both endings back to back in the nabes (jeez, I'm such an old ham. Neighborhood theaters).

Wasn't there a MURDERS IN THE RUE MORGUE that had multiple endings back-to-back, or am I hallucinating that bit of filmlore?

ROB ~

I think in the end, I'd want the cop to win and be right.

JIM ~

Me too. How about he gets to a point that he's questioning his sanity, but then stumbles upon something that leads to the real truth.

ROB ~

Like an incisor? Maybe it's huge, like a wolf's, but through DNA, it's human.

GARETH ~

And what if the cop is missing a tooth as well?

(hi guys, just another one of Alan's innumerable ragamuffins happy to find shelter in his office)

ROB ~

I think the perp should have a missing tooth but gets an implant right after the cop notices the one missing -- draws suspicion.

Maybe the "captured" incisor grows to extraordinary proportions on its own with the full moon and that's what makes the cop, finally, believable in his unbelievable pursuit.

ALAN ~

Uh ... oh boy ... WGA arbitration, here we come.

ROB ~

Enuf for a logline JK?

JIM ~

I think so. The concept could actually make for a decent low budget screen story.

ROB ~

I agree. Few characters. Mostly night shots. A few stock big city panoramic shots.

The lead character has gotta be an old guy, a detective who never quite made it. He dreams and aspires to really make it before he becomes a has-been that never-was, chasing a serial killer he thinks is a werewolf and everyone else thinks he's completely bonkers.

Maybe call it "Incisor"?

Could be the murders are taking place at a very rural locale were wolves become suspect. The problem is, it's not a pack. The victim dies by having his/her throat ripped out.

The detective is the only one on the force. He usually detects vandalism, B & E, small stuff. This is the biggest case he's had on his plate.

When he brings up "werewolf" he's thought to be bloody nuts and some suggest he should retire but he's gotta go out with a win.

He's totally alone in his belief.

ALAN ~

Yes! Small town Barney Fife vs an immortal.

Parallel action

ALAN ~

Naomi made me laugh, because she caught me evading a question and dammit it says on the front door of this shop that I'm supposed to answer questions! (so she complained, in a zmail to me). I adore her writing ability, and she had me dead to rights.

Her question was about parallel action. If memory serves, intercutting two scenes was pioneered by Edwin S. Porter a century ago. Had something to do with a train robbery and good guys chasing bad guys. Ever since then, parallel action has been used to show two or more things happening concurrently in separate locations, especially in climactic chase scenes. A spots B and gives chase. A gains on B, but B does something clever and A loses sight of him. Ah ha! There he is! Chase continues, until A finally overtakes his man and they are both in one shot together, fighting over a stick of dynamite or a rare postage stamp. Cary Grant clings to George Washington's nose at Mt Rushmore, chased by bad guys. Yawn.

Parallel action is also used in comedy. DR. STRANGELOVE (to use a recent example) cut between the War Room, Burpleson AFB, and Kong's B-52. Not a question of time shifting. Everything happened more or less continuously in multiple locales, and developments in one affected the other two, and vice versa.

I guess what I want to say about parallel action is fairly simple. There is a tendancy to overuse it. Scenes become shorter and shorter. Two on a page, three on a page, four, five, six.

If it's a chase sequence at the climax of Act Three okay. If there's an important bit of action to set up a hook at the beginning of the story okay. But I believe in the virtue of writing big meaty scenes -- 3 or 4 pages in one place without cutting away. I also believe that we should make simple pictures that tell a good story without resorting to synthetic excitement derived from parallel action.

True enough, movies became popular because the legitimate stage couldn't show us a close-up, couldn't take us to a big panorama outdoors, couldn't intercut parallel action or make a montage of angles. Those are legitimate tools of cinema.

To be used sparingly and appropriately I think. Right, Jim?

JIM ~

Below is what could well be the best parallel action sequence ever filmed. Pure genius in my opinion.

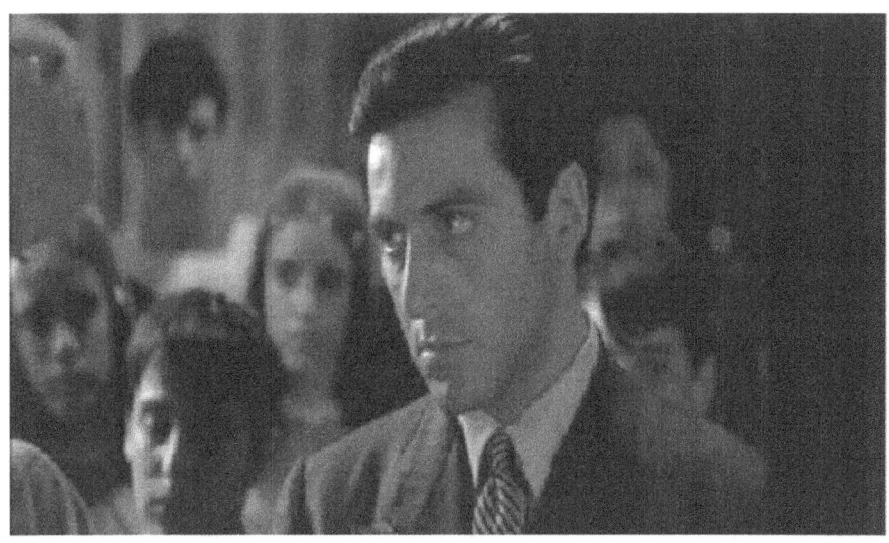

THE GODFATHER baptism scene intercut with Mafia war

ROB ~

I never had a clue how grand the company would be in this office. Thanks, Jim and Alan (and all of you). I mean, the camaraderie... the education...

NAOMI ~

Hehe, thanks Alan -- and for your zmail. Y'know, I'm more often criticised for writing scenes too long. Just for the record, there are plenty of longer scenes planned for DIZZY. But thanks for all your comments. I'll take on board everything you've said.

BRIAN ~

Scenes began getting shorter and shorter a few years back, action films especially. The reason: MTV. We had new generation of filmgoers -- the coveted youth demographic 14-24. They like video games and music videos and the trend started when you had music videos that had more edits in three minutes than most feature length films. Handheld, focus changes, crash cuts, and well, look at any of Tony Scott's films. Many of the "rules" were thrown out to cater to a perceived ADD audience. Yes, there still are solid films and even a few that do long takes that allow the actors to really shine, but you won't see many of them in "Transformers" or "Salt"

JOHN ~

I've always been struck by the power of that Godfather sequence. The juxtaposition of christening a new life in church while brutal murders are simultaneously executed is awesome. Though it's quite long, it's brilliantly held together by the sound. The scenes change visually, but the ominous church music and the priest's blessing are present throughout.

Brevity

ROB ~

I've seen scripts written like, "See Spot run. Run, Spot, run."

I do not believe this is brevity. To me, brevity has everything to do with using as few words as needed to convey the concept but not at the expense of grammar and complete sentences.

What's the standard?

ALAN ~

Generally, I draw the line at adjectives and adverbs unless they're absolutely vital -- that is: we wouldn't understand the action without quantifiers and qualifiers. No dialogue direction (dreamily) except to indicate sarcasm, irony, or business (to phone) (to Charlie).

But style is a very personal thing and we stamp our work with a signature in many ways. Criticism of structure is fairly objective. It's rare that I take issue with style of expression, if it reads well and I see the movie.

JIM ~

"What's the standard?"

The standard is brief enough that you average out to one minute of screen time per page.

In description, use key words and phrases that enable the reader to dub in the rest. Grammar, yes. Complete sentences, not necessarily.

Wordy...

INT. JOHN'S ROOM - NIGHT

There are dirty clothes thrown all about the floor, including underwear, jeans, t-shirts.

We see John's leftover dinner from the previous night, half eaten, on a plate on the desk.

Empty coke bottles are lined up against the far wall.

John is staring out the window overlooking the empty back yard.

He begins talking to himself.

>   JOHN
>   I should have gone to the party.

Less Wordy...

INT. JOHN'S ROOM - NIGHT

Not quite the messiest teenager's room in the universe.

Dirty clothes. A half eaten pizza. Empty coke bottles.

John stands at the window, staring into the lonely night.

>   JOHN
>   Should have gone to the party!

Unlike other forms, wherein we tell our story in words, in screenwriting we must tell our story in sights and sounds, since that's all we can capture on film. The idea is to get those sights and sounds to play in the theater of the reader's mind as efficiently as possible.

Too much verbiage reduces the role of the reader from active participant to mere observer... not nearly as much fun.

Overdo it word-wise and you may dilute the power of your story to the point it no longer has the impact required to create a visceral reaction in the reader. Goes from **WHAM** to *bing*. An analogy would be too much water added to a good scotch.

ALAN ~

Nice, clear as a bell. Thanks, Jim.

JAY ~

Everyone's got their style, but I would write the scene more like this:

INT. JOHN'S ROOM - NIGHT

Dirty clothes litter the floor -- underwear, jeans, t-shirts.

A plate of day-old leftovers on a cluttered desk.

Empty coke bottles line the far wall.

John stares out a window that overlooks his empty back yard.

>   JOHN
>   (to self)
>   I should have gone to the party.

Get rid of all the "are" and "is" and "ing" words you can. *"We see..."* is passive. Screenplays need to be active.

JIM ~

Nice, Jay. BTW, the second example is my actual style. I have been accused by some of being too brief.

ROB ~

Yes, getting rid of the "is...ing...are" etc. That's something I haven't been able to overcome – practice...

ALAN ~

INT. EXAMINING ROOM - DAY

BIZARRE DOCTOR enters. He never looks anyone straight in the eye and he walks with a limp. KAREN walks toward him. Attendant #2 stands up to block her way to the door. Bizarre Doctor plops a sheaf of medical records on the desk, proceeds to wash his hands at the sink.

KAREN

Are you Doctor White?

BIZARRE DOCTOR

(to Attendant)

You can go, Ronald. I'll ring if I

need you.

ATTENDANT #2

Okay, Doc.

He exits. Karen stubs out her cigarette angrily.

TONY ~

Thanks guys. As a result of the input here I'm completely revising my writing style. Agree, difficult to do. Doesn't flow as easily. Sort of like trying to change your natural golf swing. A bitch, but in the long run worth it.

ROB ~

What's that from, Alan?

ALAN ~

GOVERNOR MIKE, in the Files, sole surviving script of my career.

ROB ~

I swear, this office is like a cafe in Greenwich, smoking mota, drinking espresso, rapping with people you don't know, but hope to run into again, who wear berets.

ALAN ~

To cover up my bald spot. :-D

ROB ~

Me too... But not wanting the night to end.

Long scenes

ALAN ~

I often speak about the virtue of long scenes. Big meaty scenes in one place with continuous action. As an example of what I mean, please read pp.14-20 of Terry Southern's screenplay DR STRANGELOVE.

http://www.bibliotecah.org.uy/escribir/biblioteca/Dr.%20Strangelove.pdf

There are many long scenes in the War Room (Peter Sellers, George C. Scott) and in General Ripper's office at Burpleson AFB (Sterling Hayden, Peter Sellers).

SALLY ~

Thank you for the link and the examples, Alan. I learn well from positive examples, much more easily than from theory, so I particularly appreciate this.

BILL ~

I love this movie and I love the dialogue. First thing that comes to mind is that this screenplay would be ripped to shreds on this site for long drawn out speeches and talking heads with no action breaking it up.

Hahaha. My thoughts entirely, but it seems to me that sometimes long, talky scenes are necessary but, hey, I've had nothing produced, so what do I know?

Incidentally, not only do I agree with Alan about writing 'meaty' scenes, I believe that many actors look for them when considering a role.

ROB ~

I always like to use "Kiss of the Spider Woman" as an example of a long scene. It must have had one header, as I recall the movie.

SALLY ~

One of my favourite long scenes is in Claude Chabrol's "The Butcher" (1970). Jean Yanne and Stéphane Audran walk from the wedding through the village, talking, in an endless continuous shot. The wedding scene that precedes it is long and meaty, too.

DAVE ~

[re STRANGELOVE] - Really, one of my faves and it's been too long since I saw it last. A thinking man's film that's funny, satirical, tense, high-concept, the works. I'm going to have to buy it on DVD or Blu-Ray. Can't wait to see it again.

God, that script would get torn apart today: too much exposition, scenes too long, speeches too long, too much technical jargon, no clear protagonist with a clear goal, no character arcs, unhappy ending, etc. But look what it turned into on film, best political satire ever. Not haha funny, just clever-as-hell funny.

ALAN ~

Slim Pickens (Major Kong) on contents of survival kit: "Shoot, a feller could have a pretty good time in Vegas with all that stuff."

DAVE ~

Brilliant character. Loved him right until the end (he really went out with a bang, didn't he?)

BARRY C. ~

Slim Pickens was perfect for that role. Incredible film. If you watch Pickens deliver that line, Alan, you can see that "Vegas" was dubbed in. What Pickens actually said was "Dallas," per that version of the script.

ALAN ~

Good eye, Barry. An excellent reminder that post-production is usually 1/4 of the budget. Sign in the basement of the Australian Film Academy: "When the shooting stops, the filmmaking begins."

BARRY C. ~

Great sign! So when the screenplay is finished, the storytelling begins? Ha.

I can't claim a good eye – the DVD commentary mentioned the dubbing. Strangelove was scheduled for release the day of Kennedy's assassination: hence the dubbing and delay of the film's release to January, 1964.

ROB ~

Slim was a neighbor up here in Oregon. Having "Dallas" dubbed over pissed him off no end and he would make a point of it over barbeque and beer. But that always ended with: "If the money is green, I don't give a shit what they do with the film" – and a big smile.

His argument was Dallas was better than Vegas, and he'd detail why, mostly about the women. He had a point.

About locations

SALLY ~

Alan's talked about keeping your number of locations small. Here's a breakdown on why you want to do that, that goes into more detail:

> Write concise. The scheduling of these film shoots is an art and a thing of beauty in itself. To see your sprawling, hundred page script broken down into thirty-odd shoot days, with each scene summarised (not always to your liking) and cut up into eighth-of-a-page sections, and then these scenes grouped into non-linear production chunks according to where they are set, all ordered according to day and night and various actors' availabilities, is to get a sense of the massive endeavour that is a film shoot. It is hard, hard work, with literally hundreds of people involved. I believe they estimate (for the bonding company) on shooting between 2-3 pages a day. And every time you move location, or introduce a new actor, that costs time, which costs money. The perfect day for a film shoot is one location, a few actors, a four page scene. They can block it and rehearse it and shoot it any way they like and will probably still knock off early. The worst day is four locations, three moves, lots of cast and costume and make-up changes. Then it becomes a scramble: get it in the can. So lesson four is, as far as you can, to be concise in what you write. Can these two scenes become one? Can these two characters become one? Can this scene, at the ice rink, actually take place back at the house, where the crew will already have shot for three days, thereby saving half a day of travel and set-up? Can it go altogether? This will all involve compromise, and some rethinking of your script. But you're creative, you can figure it out. This journey of figuring out exactly what is important about any given scene – and considering whether the truly important bit can be delivered in another, maybe better, way – is a vital process in the honing of your script.

from Tom Williams on <u>Lessons in Production</u>

ALAN ~

Thanks, Sally. "Can these two characters become one? What is this scene really about? Can it play somewhere else (or go altogether)? What is the important bit?" Excellent.

SALLY ~

I'm thinking about an epic journey story these days (think Blues Brothers or Oh Brother Where Art Thou), and what I took away from this article was:

- Can I make scenes long and meaty enough to work well with a shoot schedule? i.e., aim for 4 pages.

- Can I recycle locations?

- What's the minimum number of supporting characters that will work? How much impact do I need to get from a supporting character to justify its existence?

- Given that the nature of the story dictates a lot of locations, what are other writing choices I can make to keep the cost down (that double as fresh writing choices that avoid film cliches)? – e.g., for the chase scene, the protags will be on bicycles, not in cars.

ALAN ~

I should mention the downside of "making minutes" -- long talky scenes that don't achieve much. In The Blues Brothers it was music performances (Aretha, Jake and Elwood, etc) and extravagantly expensive stunt work, for which Blues Brothers is best known. Artie Johnson, Carrie Fisher, and John Candy were used like cardboard props in a cartoon story that did everything in parody and didn't have to make sense because it was Belushi and Ackroyd.

Two-ness

ALAN ~

Occasionally I wake up in the morning with an idea. Today it's the number 2. In *First Feature*, the main character starts out with a gift of $200. The price of his first camera was $200. In the second act, he borrows $200 from his mother, and at the end of the story he has $200 in his pocket. In *Mars Shall Thunder*, a pivotal chapter is titled Two Pair -- and a deadly shoot-out begins with two pair of feet clomping down a hallway. In the third act, Laura confronts her knowledge that "Two make a fire and the embers never die."

Lewis and Clark
Rowan and Martin
Jack and Jill
two characters in Waiting For Godot
Dean Martin and Jerry Lewis
Mork and Mindy
Bonnie and Clyde

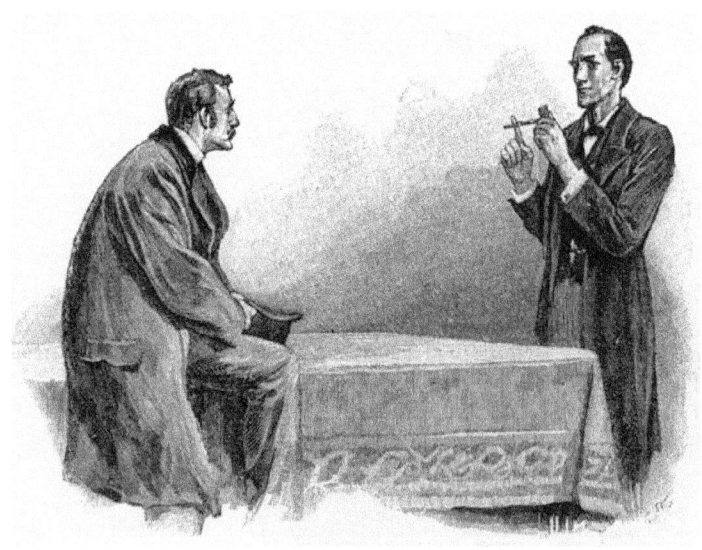

NAOMI ~

Just when I thought I was starting to run out of ideas, when I was ill and out of action recently and unable to concentrate on my real work-in-progress, I suddenly started coming up with a whole load of new stories. One of my new projects is working-titled TWO...

ALAN ~

Really made my day, Naomi. Think of you often.

ROB ~

This is actually, simply astute. Contradictions... conflicts... opposites... plus / minus... negatives / positives... the list is long.

Choices

JIM ~

A post on the main board, about folks refusing to rewrite, and a Hemingway quote about bleeding over a typewriter, got me thinking about the choices we make as writers.

Sometimes I sit down to write, and my words flow like liquid chocolate in Umpa-Lumpa Land. I think to myself, "Nothing to this writing stuff"!

What's going on? Why does it all seem so natural and perfect -- even FUN? Good writing is supposed to be hard!

Then I take a good look at my work and realize that I've seen similar stuff a million times before, and so have my potential readers. It's so familiar and so comfortable that of course it feels right -- like a very old, very well worn pair of brown shoes. When writing is that much fun for me, it's generally because I'm not doing a very good job of it -- unless of course, I'm writing the very last line of my polish draft.

Here's how it works for me…

FIRST CHOICES – Old, stale, yawn, bordering on cliché or already across the line, but easy to write.

> **BOB**
> Mom's dead, Jerry. She's gone.

Jerry comes apart. Can hardly speak. Tears stream down his cheeks.

> **JERRY**
> How… how can that be? I spoke to her on
> the phone just last night.

> BOB
> She died in her sleep. Probably a
> heart attack.

The two brothers embrace, comforting one another.

FADE TO BLACK

SECOND TRY – Feels like work, but gotta get original here!

> BOB
> Mom's dead, Jerry. She died in her
> sleep last night!

> JERRY
> Mom's d... d... dead?

Jerry faints, dead away, falls to the floor. Bob drops to his knees, and takes his brother in his arms. Jerry opens his eyes.

> BOB
> We'll get through this, big brother.
> – We will!

FADE TO BLACK

THIRD TRY – After "bleeding" over the keyboard for a while.

> BOB
> I've got really bad news.

> JERRY
> Sure you do, but give me the good
> news first.

> BOB
>
> There is no good news.
>   (beat)
> Mom's dead.

> JERRY
>   (laughing)
> Not funny!

> BOB
>
> I'm serious.

> JERRY
>
> Yeah, and I'm Roebuck. Get it? Like
> "Sears and Roebuck", only, "Serious
> and Roebuck"? And anyway, I had
> lunch with Mom just yesterday.

> BOB
>
> She died in her sleep last night. We
> don't know the cause of death yet.

> JERRY
>
> This really isn't funny, Bob!

> BOB
>
> I'm not trying to be funny! She's gone.

> JERRY
>
> FUCK YOU!

Jerry charges at his brother.
Bob backs up and falls over the coffee table. Jerry's right on him.
Grunting and groaning, the brothers wrestle around on the floor.
Bob begins to whimper... like a lost child.
Jerry's taken aback.

They stop fighting.

> **JERRY**
> Mom really is gone?

Bob breaks down into full blown tears.

> **BOB**
> Yeah.

There on the floor, Jerry holds his brother close.

> **JERRY**
> We'll get through this. Yeah. We'll
> get through this, little brother.

FADE TO BLACK

Now I have to go back and set Bob up as having a sick sense of humor so that the scene will work, but hey, that adds depth to the character, and now I've at least got a start on something original.

This is my experience. Your mileage may vary depending upon how you write.

ALAN ~

Silver Cup award for Outstanding Service to the community.

JIM ~

Hey, thanks, Alan! (Holds cup high over his head.)

DEREK ~

Always learn or view something differently from a Mr. Kalergis post.

BARRY F. ~

Just curious, Jim. A query, if you don't mind.

Your rewrite cycle here amps up the tension, the stakes, the conflict, and "incidentally" makes the characters and situation fresh and original.

I collaborated for a while with a novelist who had trouble pitching tension, stakes and conflict to the right intensity for the scene. If the pitch needed were a 7 on a 0-10 scale, she'd rewrite to a 3, and then to a 5, and then to a 6. Very laborious.

I suggested she go OTT (Over-The-Top) right on the first draft, to a 10, and then rewrite to pull it back to the needed 7. She got to the needed intensity faster that way, than with the incremental approach.

But we're amateurs, improvising; you're a pro. So I'm curious to know: do you ever go OTT and then use the rewrites to pull back rather than amp up?

JIM ~

I tend to build with each draft as appropriate, but having somebody with the problem you described go Over-The-Top early, sounds like a GREAT idea. Mind if I steal that one for my mentoring bag of tricks?

A similar thing I've noticed... Many writers tend to shy away from getting their protags in very deep or having them experience any real discomfort, possibly because it makes THEM feel uncomfortable. That uncomfortable feeling is called "dramatic tension." Dramatic tension is good!

Part of my approach is to play off my characters' contrasting needs in order to build dramatic tension.

For instance, in the little sample scene I wrote:

Bob <u>needs</u> to tell Jerry that their mom has passed away, and he <u>needs</u> to be "the strong one" in this time of family crisis. Jerry <u>needs</u> NOT to get that his mother is really dead. In the end, they both <u>need</u> each other, and Jerry <u>needs</u> to be the strong one.

ALAN ~

I've had a completely different experience with comedy. My first drafts tended to be "too much movie" and a little chaotic. The storyline was there, but it needed to be cut down to size (less $), add depth, clean up clunky exposition. With straight drama I always did the Scene Card work first, then wrote a tight first-and-final draft and pitched it for production. A production deal involves a script doctor and open heart surgery. Writers hate it. Directors love it.

Not entirely sure why anyone should write three drafts of anything. On the set I was opposed to shooting more than four or five takes. The first take was often the best, but you do a couple more for protection. Occasionally there was an improv that required re-making or tossing out previous work already in the can.

Best practice I believe is to write something, leave it alone for a year, see it with fresh eyes, do the Scene Card workflow and craft a good final draft -- or abandon it and write something else.

Toying and tinkering with endless versions doesn't seem right.

ROB ~

For me, after writing the first draft and let's say I'll be doing an errand and a scene or a change in a scene comes to mind. I always have a notebook. So then I'll rewrite that scene. For instance (from Magic Show rewrite) in an abusive orphan asylum, I have this young teenager being beat on the back with a switch, then locked up in a stand-up cabinet in the basement. From the time he comes on screen, he seems like a toughy, and he is, in public.

Then I had this idea. He's in the closet, alone, it's dark, save for light from a full moon coming through high windows and I have this tough kid try to choke off whimpers and maybe softly sing "Jesus loves me... this I know..." between whimpers, off key.

And for me, I could have such an idea and make the change, and changes made there could force a re-think and change either earlier or later.

In the above, when a friend brings him a bowl of rice and beans, sees the streaks (from tears) marking his cheeks, astonished, says, "You've been crying!" or some such. Unlike life, as a story-teller, I get to change the past, present and future until I'm in love with all of it.

Real good to meet you here. You've taught me a lot.

BARRY F. ~

Alan, just babbling here, but when Se7en came out, I was so blown away that I read every version of Walker's script, just to see what rewrites were all about. I no longer remember the details, but I remember my sense of disappointment. As far as I could tell, what Walker seemed to have put his rewrite energy into was moving a scene down a slot and then back again (when it worked as well in either place) and changing a mundane line to another version of a mundane line. I couldn't fathom what he was doing. To my ignorant eyes, it just looked as if he didn't know what a rewrite was for, but he was doing it anyway. I guess I expected mastery or something. Ha! Se7en is an incredible script and film. Talk about coming up with a fresh take on the hackneyed old buddy movie.

Script Doctoring 101

JIM ~

Bill asked me to post something about my "script doctoring" approach to rewriting. This at once takes us into the world of screen story analysis, and that's really a book, not a blurb on an Internet discussion board. That said, I'll do my best to give you an overview of the most important part of the process… analyzing a story's basic structure. I don't know that there's any official, correct way to go about analyzing the structure of a screen story, but what follows is my basic approach, and it works for me every time.

It wouldn't make much sense, and you wouldn't get much of an end result, if you just dived in and began rewriting a screenplay without first figuring out the existing structure of the piece, and sorting out what's missing, and what should and shouldn't be there.

Just as you can analyze a sentence by breaking it down into its parts of speech, you can analyze a screen story by breaking it down into its "through-lines." There are other workable structures but most screenplays have one major through-line, which runs from start to finish, and a couple of minor through-lines that run within the body of the story, either intersecting or running parallel to the major through-line. The major through-line belongs to the protagonist. The minor through-lines belong to supporting players. I hope I'm not getting too technical here and putting everyone to sleep!

"What the hell is a through-line?" you might ask. The easiest way to understand the concept is to think of a through-line as a "dramatic question."

The major through-line poses the start-to-finish <u>central dramatic</u> question. The minor through-lines pose <u>lesser dramatic questions.</u>

For example:

THE WIZARD OF OZ
CENTRAL DRAMATIC QUESTION (Major Through-line)
"Will Dorothy find her way safely back to Kansas or fall victim to the wicked witch?"

That question is what the story is mostly about. Act 1 is about setting up and posing the question. Act 2 is about exploiting the question and keeping the audience guessing how it will be answered. Act 3 is about satisfactorily answering the question.

THE WIZARD OF OZ
LESSER DRAMATIC QUESTIONS (Minor Through-lines)
"Will the Scarecrow get a brain?"
"Will the Tin Man get a heart?"
"Will the Cowardly Lion find his courage?"

In this case the lesser through-lines run parallel to the major through-line. Once you've identified the story's through-lines you'll know what's MISSING from the story.

1) Is there no viable major through-line, or central dramatic question even posed?

2) Is the through-line not strong enough or well set up enough to suck the reader in?

3) Is there not enough opposition inherent in the setup to generate the twists, turns, obstacles, and reversals necessary to fully exploit the central dramatic question in Act 2?

4) Is the central dramatic question well answered? Is there enough of a pay-off for the reader/audience to feel they got their time and money's worth?

Repeat the process above for each of the lesser through-lines, and you'll have a pretty good picture of the structural condition of the piece.

Once you've identified the story's through-lines, you'll also know what DOESN'T belong. With the exception of the very occasional comic relief scene, or scene just for pacing purposes, <u>every line of every scene should move the story forward along one of its through-lines.</u> If it doesn't, what's it doing there?

Of course there's much more to a full analysis, but the above is a quick and dirty way to get a handle on a story's basic structure, and a good idea of what you need to do to fix or improve it. Who was the famous sculptor who said all he does is cut away everything that doesn't look like a horse?

NAOMI ~

If I may...

I find Paul Chitlik's book REWRITE useful. He identifies seven distinct points that each throughline must have. The major throughline's plot points dictate the overall structure of the movie, of course. The minor throughlines may be shorter and paced differently but should still have all seven points in order.

1 - Ordinary life
2 - Inciting incident
3 - Call to action (end of act one for the main throughline, when the character chooses a course of action, or is forced to get involved)
4 - New direction (midpoint, when things take an unexpected turn and the goal may change or take on new meaning)
5 - Low point (all is lost, end of act two)
6 - Final challenge (a new call to action at the beginning of act three)
7 - Return to normal life (now changed forever)

I thought I knew all that stuff already, but until I actually sat down to restructure one of my stories I didn't realise that some of my plot points weren't clear enough.

JIM ~

Hi Naomi,

I've seen maybe a half-dozen versions of this, and they are useful. They're all the end result of studying the patterns commonly found in good screenplays.

Christopher Vogler broke new ground in 1993 with his book, "The Writers Journey: Mythic Structure for Writers." I think he was the first to describe such a pattern, although his work is based upon an earlier, less popular and less readable book.

There's a caution anybody using these plot point patterns needs to be aware of. Well-structured screenplays tend to follow these patterns, but incorporating such a pattern is no guarantee of workable structure.

Why? Because these are the end results of putting together a good story, not the starting points.

If you tell a good story without any attention to structure, chances are it will generally conform to one of these common patterns. For instance, you'll start with "ordinary life" because that's the first step in setting up your major through-line. You've got to get the reader or audience to connect with your protagonist via their ordinary life, or they won't give a damn what happens to him or her. If you force it into place, after the fact, without realizing why it occurs so regularly in good stories, it may not work.

Another example:

The act 1 turning point, or what Chitlik called "call to action" is also a naturally occurring event. Why? Because it takes that long to set up and pose your central dramatic question. Once that question is posed you move into a new phase... the protagonist's efforts to see that the central dramatic question is answered to his liking, and the antagonists efforts against him or her.

My point is that you can't just superimpose these things on your screenplay in rewrite and expect the result to be a better screenplay. When you see one of the events is missing or out of place, you have to ask yourself "why?" and deal with the reason it's missing or out of place. Find where you originally went wrong and fix it, rather than adding something new.

Example:

There's no inciting incident around page 7. Why? Is the inciting incident on page 20? If so, why is my story starting so late? Did I include unnecessary back-story in my setup? Did I wander around aimlessly?

Or maybe there's no midpoint. Do I need one? Does the story slump mid act 2? Did I fail to raise the stakes where I should have? Was there not enough inherent conflict in my story to begin with? Do I need a more powerful antagonist?

Get the idea?

Story structure must stem from your characters' needs, wants, desires, and the situations they find themselves, and that won't happen if you just blindly follow ones of these plot patterns while hoping for the best.

So yes, these structure patterns can be very useful, but you need to think with them. You can't arbitrarily plug each one in by page number and expect the end result to be a well structured story.

BILL ~

Jim, thank you for this; I appreciate your help and advice. Very helpful indeed; I will print this out as as a 'keeper.'

Yours aye.

ROB ~

Too many script doctors and "experts" are like those who've learned the tune but have never spent any time in the trenches making a living at it. Even McKee, who I think is brilliant, but is confusing and someone who could make you improve... maybe.

I'd rather listen to someone who makes a living by writing or producing. A script doctor is a know-best, yet has never put a worthy idea into silver bromide. He's a doctor who's never operated. He's a parrot. He can't help me.

FRANK ~

Is a script doctor the same as, similar to, or meant to serve the same purpose as a book doctor?

JIM ~

I'm not familiar with what book doctors do, Frank. I guess the basic idea is that script doctors diagnose and heal sick screenplays, often on the set. I believe those who do specialized rewrite work in the motion picture industry just call themselves writers.

Aaron Sorkin, for example, is often brought onto a set and makes HUGE money cleaning up dialog. Nobody calls him a Script Doctor. Same with John Milius. He's brought in to rewrite scenes that aren't working.

As Julie pointed out, there are so-called "script doctors" floating around offering their services to newbies. I would be leery of them without a strong recommendation from somebody I trusted.

ROB ~

And like I mentioned before, how could one trust a character who hasn't written (in a number of genres), sold and had their screenplays produced, more than a few times

I find it amazing how it's full of aspiring writers and then a great number of others who exploit and take advantage of them -- like "Script Doctors" and screenplay contests. I seriously doubt Sorkin, Millus, Kalergis or a good writer would enter film contests or pay hundreds of dollars to have their scripts doctored.

The ideal scene would be a writer competent to fix his/her own work, after all, that's part of a screenwriter's job description.

JIM ~

That is the ideal, Rob.

The problem is that our work is always perfect. Why would we write it any other way? That's why we can all benefit from a professional evaluation of our work before we call the script a done deal. There's something to be said for a fresh set of eyes with a person behind those eyes who understands how screenplays work.

Teaching/coaching/mentoring takes an entirely different skill set from doing, so I wouldn't rule out non-writer readers and analysts entirely. Scott Mullen, for example, has covered about 9,000 studio scripts. He's got to have learned a few things in the process. Same with my pal, Lynne Pembroke.

ROB ~

Points well made and taken, Jim.

Marketing

Suggested characters, locales, themes

ALAN ~

As I mentioned elsewhere recently, don't remember precisely which thread, I believe it's important to write spec screenplays that can be produced for less than $10 million. That sounds like a lot of money, until you consider the fixed costs ("below the line") of a 35mm feature film.

Completion bonding, production insurance, accounting, legal, interest expense, office expense, FICA, workers comp, sales tax, and contingency allowance are roughly **20% of budget** -- and we haven't shot anything yet. Overhead G&A expenses scale up on bigger projects. Studio pictures get socked with front office overheads. That's why "little" studio pictures cost $15+ million. But let's stick with an indie feature and negative pick-up deal from a distributor and/or TV network.

Raw stock and laboratory is going to eat another **20% of budget**. A 100-minute movie in 35mm is 9,000 ft of film. Allow 100,000 ft of raw stock, processing all of it, printing about a third, two internegs and a timed answer print, editing facilities, video transfers, ADR, Foley, sound mastering, projection, and half a dozen release prints for festivals and trade screenings. Still haven't shot the movie.

Camera rentals, grip equipment, lighting, generator, sound stage, location expense, honey wagon, police permits, transportation, mileage, per diems, air travel expense, taxis, parking tickets, a couple production co-ordinators and truck rentals will ding another **15% of budget**. Still haven't shot the movie. We don't even have a crew yet. Let's add another **5% of budget** for "below the line" operator, sound mixer, boom man, focus puller, clapper loader, grips, electricians, standby painter, set decorator, make-up and hair, prop man, publicist.

60% of the budget gone -- for fixed costs.

Then we come to the variable "above the line" circus. Did you expect the producer to work for free? He/she needs an associate producer, a production manager, unit manager, casting director, expense account: **10% of budget.**

How about director, 1st asst director, 2nd asst (to manage the extras), script supervisor, film editor, asst editor, sound editor? Need a top notch DP and his assistant? Music? -- another **10% of budget.**

Screenplay, script doctor, research, title clearance? **5% of budget**

Actors? Supporting cast? Bits and extras? Pensions? **10% of budget**

Art department, sets, wardrobe, props, clean-up... **5% of budget**

Imagine how hard this is to do super-cheap. Everything gets whacked. No Panavision, no sets, no stars.

For this reason, I'll suggest locales, characters, and themes that make sense for small movies:

Antartic lab in a snowstorm
Old mansion
Luxury condo/apartment
Tahoe hunting lodge
Family farm

The idea here is keep the action more or less contained in a geographically compact area. There is a Western street at the Disney Ranch you can use, provided you don't load it up with horses, wagons, barroom brawls and whatnot. Keep it simple.

Mad scientist
Sheriff
Young couple
Old woman
A fugitive

I don't like downbeat stories personally, and they are a tough sell in some TV markets. However the main idea is to pick one or two main characters that an A-list star might be tempted to portray. Jack Palance did Percy Adlon's BAGDAD CAFE, for instance.

Redemption
Reunion
Experiment
Discovery
Love

If you're writing a drama, put some comedy in it, and vice versa. Think texture. No animation please.

SALLY ~

Thank you for taking the time to write this all up, Alan.

There's a lot of information out there (now) about "how to write", but not how to write with business considerations in mind.

I really appreciate the light that you and others here can shed on how writing with an eye to keeping costs down, to making directors and producers happy, etc.

BRIAN ~

Permit me to add to Alan's list:

How to make a low budget feature producer happy...

Small cast
No children
No animals
No explosions
No car chases, crashes, specialty cars

No period pieces
No "on-the-water" scenes
No digital special effects
Few locations, centrally located
100 page, original script
No aerials (helicopter, plane)
No cranes, or special equipment (i.e. steadycam, underwater)
Use existing (practical) structures for sets.

Now you can see why horror films are the producer's easiest genre to pull off on a low budget.

Hockey mask $25.00
Bucket of blood $50.00
Budget under a million: Priceless

p.s. - I've never shot one film that adheres to the above list. ;-)

ALAN ~

Brian is more in touch with today's prices and production methods. I always appreciate his input, any topic.

What got me thinking about this was Matt Voss' spec screenplay KISS OFF. Superb comedy. Almost flawless. I estimated $50 million. Who is going to gamble $50 million on a comedy? and where do we get a beautiful young Olympic gymnast to double for a beautiful young Russian actress (love interest)?

One more idea on this subject. My first screenplay was a blockbuster. Had great fun letting my imagination soar. Rewrote it years later. Never sold.

My first screenwriting assignment was for an action movie budgeted at $1 million (in today's money it would be $2 million) to be shot on location in Mexico.

My first feature as writer-director was shot on Super16. It saved $50,000 compared to shooting 35mm. There was no completion bond and it was never completed. We ran out of money, because the producer authorized a budget slightly higher than the pre-sale cash he had in hand.

Moral of the story: The fees I got paid for screenwriting went from $0 (spec blockbuster) to $5,000 (first assignment) to $30,000 (my low budget 16mm first feature). There were more spec scripts and more work-for-hire assignments.

I always made money on assignment.

SALLY ~

Alan, is there any sense in writers today writing a blockbuster as a spec script? Not as a first script, obviously. But if a writer is already writing and selling specs, could it make sense at that point?

Or are blockbusters currently written on assignment? or by writer-directors?

ALAN ~

Jim and Brian need to balance what I'm about to say. The only purpose in writing a spec script is to have something to show, to introduce yourself to agents, producers, and actors who are involved in deals that lead to writing work-for-hire. I met a lot of established, successful and respected writers in Hollywood. They were all angling for another assignment, a deal based on personal professional contacts and a concept, rather than a spec screenplay. They were represented by agents who were trying to get them hired.

Keep in mind that my film career was cut short, and I had to start over in TV, after my first feature blew up in my face. A few spec scripts have sold -- LITTLE MISS SUNSHINE, GRAN TORINO – small movies, not blockbusters.

Wendy Henson has written some great spec scripts. To the best of my knowledge, none were produced. They were optioned and "packaged" and that was as far as it went. I don't think Wendy pursued work-for-hire, but that's speculation on my part. I invited her to the Office and she declined.

SALLY ~

In light of that, what would you consider to be the criteria for a good spec script as a writing sample? Write with passion, write with craft, write to budget? -- i.e., demonstrate unteachables, teachables, and business savvy. Anything else?

ALAN ~

Personal suggestion: write what you love to write. It's honest, you'll enjoy the work, be glad to show it, and if a deal comes from it (representation, etc) you can look at yourself in the mirror each morning and smile about it.

JIM ~

Yes, the chances of selling a big budget spec script are pretty slim. In any give year, you can count the number of specs that get made and gain wide distribution on one hand, and in some years on one finger.

But here's the conundrum... An informal survey of pros on another site revealed that for the vast majority of writers it takes 6 to 10 efforts to really come up to speed, craft-wise. If an aspiring writer doesn't write on spec, how will he or she ever get good at the game?

Rarely is there any financial reward for our early efforts. What we do get, if we really work at it, is EXPERIENCE and KNOW HOW. For all that time and effort we make a bit of forward progress on the learning curve, and that does have value.

If you don't look back on your early scripts and think they suck, you're either not making much progress, you're delusional, or you're that one in a million "natural." I've only met one "natural" ever. As for delusional... well, I won't go there.

Eventually, after much time and hard work, the learning curve does finally flatten out, but I don't think we ever really stop learning.

The usual path for pro writers is that they use a spec as a writing sample to get assignment work. In the process of writing on assignment, they open doors to possible future spec sales.

There's also the low budget spec market, where newbies face much better odds, but there's not much money there.

If you're serious about screenwriting, it's a good idea to have a game plan of one kind or another. Figure out where you want to get to, and then work backwards from there. And don't sweat the competition. There's nowhere near as much competition out there as you might think.

All that said, now and again, against all odds, lightning strikes! A few years back a friend of mine and her writing partner sold their very first screenplay for $250,000 advance against $500,000.

BARRY C. ~

I'm currently writing a script that I hate. It's absolute drudgery to drag my sorry a** over the computer and continue to write it. I took the commission as a favour to a producer who I've already done a fair bit of work for. Even he was pushing it to me as "we'll just grit our teeth, make the movie, and take the paycheque" (oops - paycheck for my American friends). As for the reason I hate it... It's a movie based on one of my pitches, but the two executive producers -- new to the industry -- had all their "wonderful" ideas and a whole list of changes they wanted which made it a just a bad storyline with all the things I dislike in any movie. As my producer says, it's their money. It may be their money, but it's my face I have to look at in the mirror each day. Lesson learned, never take a job just for the money.

I'm honestly thinking of sending this one out under a nom de plume.

ROB ~

Hey, Barry, good to meet you. I cringe imagining your situation.

Where's the love? IMHO, money's never good enuf if there's no passion, just my opinion. Your story sounds like committing hari kari because a good friend asked you to, and you feel you owe him.

BARRY C. ~

He's not necessarily a good friend, but like any "vendor" I don't want him (essentially my "customer") going to the competition to buy another product -- if you know what I mean.

Even when writing a spec as a writing sample, keep budget in the back of your mind. For example, it doesn't matter how many scenes you have... just locations. Moving to another location eats up money and shooting days in the schedule. So if you can re-use a location, hopefully in a way where it either looks or feels different, by all means show that you can save money in a creative fashion.

Writing with budget in mind is also good practice for the first assignments you get which will probably be of the lower budget variety. So far I've had the good fortune to get assignments from a couple of producers up here in Canada and quite frankly I think one of the reasons they pick up the phone and call me first for their next project is because I write to their budget and manage to fill their wish lists. One guy will give me a list of locations he has access to, a list of actors he wants to use, budget for effects, and the discussions can even go so far as shooting days in the schedule and how many days he can afford certain actors for certain parts.

He'll also give me a very general idea of what kind of story he's looking for. I then take his wish list and come up with a concept storyline and write him a pitch or treatment with which he goes and secures the funds to commission the script. After that, we're off to the races!

It's only lower budget direct-to-DVD/TV release films, and I'm not sure just how common this little system is elsewhere in the industry, but it seems to be working okay up here. Actually, maybe some of you could let me know if this is anywhere near the way it works south of the border.

ALAN ~

American TV movies were an important business years ago, not so much now, although HBO, Showtime, Hallmark, Turner and others still commission indie made-for-cable. The financial equation hasn't changed. Producers get something upfront, have to make DVD and foreign sales to break even.

A report from the trenches

ALAN ~

"Irate Reader-Writer" kindly supplied a discussion thread on the Main board that caught my attention: How to pitch. She seems convinced that email is a good idea.

She also disparaged a personal contact at Shepperton that I gave her and mischaracterized what happened in reality. I suggested that she contact an agent of my acquaintance, not Branaugh's production company. I also told "Irate" that she had to go to London and be introduced in person. That was five years ago.

In today's MB discussion, it was asserted that my old fashioned idea of Who Knows Who and personal contacts in Hollywood is silly and kaput. The implication was personal introductions don't matter any more, and email queries are the correct way to pitch a script.

... WTF?

TOM ~

I don't think anyone was saying personal contacts were bad, Alan. If you don't have personal contacts, calling is the best route. Calling generally leads to an email address and a request for the logline. That is all. You send it in. The person of interest reads it and if they like it, then it goes somewhere or not.

Personal contacts aren't possible for the screenwriter living in Bumfuck, World. The best they can get is a friendly talk with the receptionist, usually. If you are lucky, you'll actually get the said agent, manager, or producer on the line and have a decent phone conversation with them.

However, I see "Irate" was freaking out a bit. She can't call for whatever her reason. She obviously does not know how to react to dealing with a receptionist. People aren't the devil in Hollywood. You just have to be polite to them and they are usually helpful. You get the email address of how the place in question takes submissions and you send in your loglines. That is how it works for most agents, managers, and production companies today. If you are lucky enough to actually have a personal contact, then you can talk to that person on the phone.

ALAN ~

I'm just old and cranky. You have the right approach, Tom. Phone 'em up, ask for the boss. Not there? Okay, please tell him/her I called. When's a good time to reach him/her? I have a project I want to pitch.

Eventually you get through.

TOM ~

Alan, that is an even better phone approach than I currently use. I usually bow out to the receptionist's wall that says "Hey, you can submit your logline here." It would be better to get past the receptionist and actually talk with the agent or manager or producer.

CHRIS K. ~

I email.

I get no response, or "send me your script," or "send your script to so and so and tell them I asked for it."

I figure any way you can get reads, get them.

ALAN ~

The other thing that makes sense is to qualify people you want to talk to. Do some research. Agents: Who do they represent? (writers? directors? what kind of movies?) Producers: What films have they made? Google and IMDb the boss' name. Have a positive specific reason for calling him/her and have something to talk about.

I want to send you a blockbuster set in ancient Mesopotamia. You're the only guy who can do it justice - or - I have a love story I want you to read, because you did FENTON ON ACID.

"Irate" is barking up the wrong tree pitching actor managers. Writers do not sell scripts to actors.

Chris, I'm sure you're doing a good job. I'm sure you're keeping track of each contact and doing follow-up. I'm sure your work is registered with the Guild or LOC. You kept a record of who got copies of your script(s) and a post office/UPS receipt for insured or 2nd day ground or something like that.

Have you had any correspondence in reply?
Received calls from an agent or producer to discuss your work?
Have you sold anything, I mean for real money?

Not trying to put you on the spot. My worry is that there's no copyright on ideas. Why let somebody read your ideas, unless you know who it is and what their agenda is? Somebody mentioned 400 producers with published email addresses. How many movies and what kind of movies have they produced? Why are they reading spec scripts?

Tell me you're not sending pdfs. Please.

My whole thing is to *identify* who you want to work with and a positive reason for pitching them in particular. Not just William Morris or CAA, but a particular agent at the agency because _____.

ROB ~

What's the deal or not, about sending PDFs?

ALAN ~

How would you ever prove it was sent or received or forwarded to someone else?

ROB ~

Because the properties are not included? What?

ALAN ~

Help me here, Jim, if you're on deck, please.

ROB ~

Am I too stupid?

ALAN ~

Not at all, Rob. Let's hang out and see what Kalergis thinks. I may be all wet.

ROB ~

Gotcha.

CHRIS K. ~

I have a spreadsheet with all contacts. These are vetted agents and managers. I've only pitched a handful of prodco's.

Anything I send out is registered with the WGAw and copyrighted. All copies of emails are retained and filed digitally.

To date I've not received any follow up beyond read requests. I have gotten polite responses, but no money or offers.

This isn't the middle ages of email 1993. If there is a digital 'sent' file with pdf attached that's pretty much proof the email was sent and received. They can even look at whether you've actually read the email now, so there's no more "I didn't get that email" malarky.

TOM ~

Alan, I can't speak for others but researching a particular agent is fairly easy in the modern world. You just log onto Done Deal Pro and see the latest script sales of a particular agent or manager. And then you go to IMDb Pro and see who that particular agent represents. It gives you a pretty good idea of who is a real player and who isn't.

ALAN ~

I'm such an old fossil, sheesh. Went in and shook hands with people, face to face.

TOM ~

My experience is pretty similar to Chris's experience though I bet he started before me and has more. Chris is spot on. I don't have a spreadsheet like Chris, but I know who I sent my loglines too because I have an email record. I am just working my way down the list of managers now. I've contacted the As and Bs of the ones I want to contact. Not all the As and Bs are reputable so I just skip contacting them. Chris' spreadsheet sounds more organized than my method, but my method is just as safe and works for me.

I've got 'Janissary' and 'Capture The Flag' being read by one reputable management firm that manages an actress that starred on the SOCIAL NETWORK. They have some other good clients and a decent track record of script sales. They are just a small boutique management firm, but they are exactly what I am looking for. I got the two reads from the same manager by doing the method I just described above.

ALAN ~

I think I'll just sit at my desk and read quietly for a day or two.

TOM ~

Don't do that. We love your comments, Alan.

BTW, I think that management firm is going to pass on me. I haven't heard back from them in two weeks. However, I am not worried about that. I will keep on trucking and getting more reads. I plan on calling and emailing about 400 managers listed on Done Deal Pro. I won't contact all of them of course because many of them are bottom feeders or don't have any recent sales. However, there will still be enough left on the list of 400 managers to get more than a few reads of Janissary and/or Capture The Flag. I average about 1 read per 10 calls/emails. My responses have been like Chris's. You either hear nothing, or please send the script, or send the script to so and so.

JIM ~

I'm not a fan of email queries or of sending files electronically. To my way of thinking, email is for selling counterfeit Viagra, not diamonds or other valuable commodities like brilliant screenplays. As for de-livery... overnight or messenger delivered hard copies are the only way to go. Act like you're selling a 5-carat diamond. Qualify your prospect. But maybe that's just me. I understand some have done okay with email queries and pdf files.

TOM ~

Jim, I do wonder about sending in a printed script versus a PDF file. I am not worried about the safety of them because there really is no safety if someone is a determined thief. However, you can get a sense of whether someone is a flake or phoney based upon who they represent and whether they've had any real sales.

Anyway, I asked the manager that requested the script whether he wanted hard copy or pdf. He preferred pdf. What that means, I could read into it a thousand scenarios, but I tend to believe a pdf was just more convenient for the company and him.

I guess what I'm wondering is... to me, a printed script just seems more valuable than a pdf. However, I can also see the value and ease of a pdf too. A pdf can be transferred around an office to various people within the office easier than copying multiple copies of a script. I can read a pdf just as easily as a hard copy script, maybe even easier, but then I'm from the tech saavy generation :)

I don't know if I am doing right by sending in a pdf. I think I will continue to ask an agent or manager whether they prefer hard copy or pdf. However, any thoughts are appreciated.

JIM ~

I prefer hard copies because there's actually something there. :)

Might be a generational thing, but I would much rather read a hard copy. Given the choice, I would opt to send a hard copy over a PDF file. On the other hand, when I'm doing analysis work, if I start with a hard copy, I scan it to a file so I can cut and paste excerpts into my notes. Seems to me the best practice is to give them what they want. Those likely to pass a script around could be more likely to go the pdf route... or maybe they just find them easier to dispose of. :)

Maybe if the request is via email, a pdf is expected in return?

In my original post [above] I was thinking more about requests made in person or by phone.

TOM ~

I know. I fear the "Delete" key :) Seriously though, I think I will just ask them what they want and give it to them. Making life easier on them is what we should do as writers because it makes us easier people to work with, which is important to those agents, managers, and producers of the future.

Thanks for your thoughts, Jim. It makes it clearer on what I should do. From my limited calling experience, they all seem to want the logline in email format. I think it is so they can read and review the logline before they leap into a read. I have just started asking the receptionist what their submission policy is. 10 out of 10 has been an emailed logline. They don't want to mess with you on the phone until they've read the script.

STEPHAN ~

Not sure if you have heard anything about a website called "Writer's little black book?" If anybody has had an experience with this group I would be interested to hear good stories/bad stories. The idea behind the procedure is you pitch a one sheet by fax. They provide the list of prodco's with a fax # and the person to contact. Apparently worked for the guy who started the company (name escapes me right now.) I am going to pitch my comedy through the list provided on the website.

TOM ~

I haven't heard of that particular service. However, it sounds like a lesser version of InkTip or VirtualPitchFest. You can try those services if you want. However, I prefer having control over where my script does or does not go. I am not pitching production companies right now. I am pitching agents and managers so when the time is right they can help me shape a marketing plan for my script -- get it on the right desks at the right time when the script is the best it can be. Even if I don't sell Janissary and Capture The Flag, I hope they leave a good taste in the mouths of my readers and lead to future jobs.

By the way, you can post in the forums section of Done Deal Pro in the agents and managers threads. There you can ask others about "Writers' little black book." Someone there might have a personal story to tell. However, I don't personally like the idea of my loglines going out to people that I don't know and haven't researched. That's just me, though. The reason I don't want my loglines going wide is because the bottom feeders and wackos and phonies of Hollywood will come out of the woodwork and waste my time.

RLB ~

Writers do not sell scripts to actors. May I qualify that with "unless the actor is dying to be a producer/director."

ALAN ~

An actor who wants to direct can be approached, possibly on con-ingent or deferred fee, but you have to pay him. Still need the money. And it's important to consider carefully the fact that most producers have no money. They're looking for a payday themselves, from pre-sales, investors, or a bankable studio deal.

Holy crap! What do I do?

NAOMI ~

The first guy to read ABCDE (a director) loved it and wants to take it to his producer!

I feel so naive about this stuff - I just don't know how to handle it. He wants to know what sort of responses I've had so far (none) and how many people I've sent it to (just four others).

I don't know what to tell him and I don't know how much I'm supposed to play the field, or whether I just run with this...

I do wanna get it produced. I don't wanna get walked on. I do think the script has a lot of commercial appeal. I don't see how I'm gonna get anyone with money to read it (sick of seeing the words 'no unsolicited submissions')!

I feel like such a moron. Why don't they tell you how to do this stuff in the books, huh?

SALLY ~

Naomi, I'll let wiser heads than mine give you good advice here. Just wanted to say Congratulations! Enjoy this moment. I hope it's the beginning of a new wave of success for you.

ROB ~

Naomi, WAY TO GO! ... I told you when I read your script that it would probably do well and I still believe that. Breath deep, clear your mind... the answers come to mind when everything is clear.

ALAN ~

Responding to your initial post. Haven't read the other replies yet.

Do you personally like this guy (the director)?

If yes, let him run with it, cash money on the table, please.
If you haven't met him in person, request a meeting.
If you *have* met him and distrust him for any reason, back out.

ABCDE is his ticket to stardom. More than the director, success or failure depends on the producer. Price yourself high enough to make it hurt. You want to see a TV presale and cash on the table upfront.

If it looks like a contract is forthcoming, hire a lawyer (not an agent or manager) to negotiate on your behalf.

Big smooches. Stay calm.

JIM ~

Looking at his IMDb history, I would say this director is still in the "aspiring" category. That is, he hasn't yet broken into the everyday, working world of the motion picture industry. Nothing wrong with that, but don't expect a lot of cash up front from him. Expect more of a partnership relationship.

My advice would be that you find out what his plans are for the script and go from there. Maybe he has some good contacts, and the fact that he actually completed a feature, counts for something.

CHRIS K. ~

The only thing I can say is deal with him like you would any business relationship.

NAOMI ~

The producer loved it too; they want to option it with the intention of going into production later this year!

We've exchanged a lot of emails and from everything I've seen and heard, they're nice people with big plans and a lot of contacts. And they're really excited about the script.

I'm meeting with them next week to hear more about their plans and "discuss the possibility of optioning" the script. This will be my first contact with anyone in the business and I have no idea what to expect. Anyone got any tips?

Is there anything I should prepare or take with me? Any questions I should ask?

RLB ~

Take notes, listen carefully, and stay calm. Don't sign anything until you've had a chance to read over it away from distractions.

ALAN ~

Naomi. Listen. Carefully. Make them say Ouch!

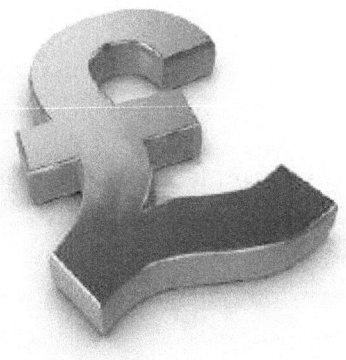

ROB ~

Alan is right. If they say ouch and then don't want it they didn't really want it in the first place. If they really do, they'll negotiate.

TOM ~

If they don't have a lot of money upfront for you, you could always go with Gross Points in the film. Some people like all their money upfront. However, if you think the producers don't have enough money to make you happy, then consider Gross Points... avoid Net Points because you will never see a dollar with Net Points. I would not ask beyond one or two Gross Points. Some big writers get Gross points. I know one Writer/Producer that has several Gross points written into her contract. However, remember, she is also a producer so her contract is a little different.

ALAN ~

Absolutely not. No points. Period.

Not even with completion bonding, a presale, and a w.k. star.

Sorry, Tom. No.

ROB ~

Tom, that's a real good example of "them" getting something (the script) and giving Naomi nothing. That's NOT good business. It is unethical and even though many do it, doesn't mean it's right. Many doing it means many are doing bad business.

TOM ~

It is your choice to make, Alan. You can take your pay day upfront. Or you can risk the film never gets made, never makes a profit, and all the other risks, yet still take Gross points on the hope that if your film gets made and is successful you will make money.

It is a personal choice. Risk versus reward. Most screenwriters take the money and run.

ROB ~

With all due respect, Tom, I think my goal as a writer is to write the best script I can and I feel certain that's all writers' primary goal. IMHO it's not a risk or loss if it never gets made. I find it extremely irresponsible if I subject my story to being produced and I don't get paid. I'd never sell screen rights I own for nothing but a promise.

Chris talks about good business. Where can you buy something and not pay for it?

JIM ~

Given we don't know [the production company's] situation or intentions, I would suggest any advice to Naomi is a bit premature...

The usual case with these guys is that they need a good script in order to begin the fundraising process. It's a Catch 22 for them.

Once Naomi has all the facts, she'll need to make her decision based upon those facts -- but it ain't like she's being chased around the block by MGM and Fox.

184

TOM ~

Good point, Jim. I'm sorry I said anything. I just know most of the independent producers don't have enough money to pay upfront for a good script. I was aware that the producer will likely use the good script to raise funds. It is a question of whether Naomi believes in this producer as hard-working, hands on, and with lots of good financing and talent contacts that can make this story into a film with a reasonable budget. If she doesn't believe in him, it is a case of take the money you can get and run or just walk away and hope for a better deal sometime in the future.

NAOMI ~

Oi! No fighting on my thread!

Thanks everyone for your input.

You know, it's the stuff other than money that's bothering me most. I'd like to keep sole writing credit, maybe get involved with production wherever I can, see what else I can get out of the experience. I don't know what the standard is or what'll be expected of me.

ALAN ~

Standard deal:

Two revisions to satisfaction of producer
Written by and/or "original screenplay by" credit
Shared "screenplay by" if they hire another writer

Personal advice, don't go near the set.

ROB ~

I agree, Tom, not fighting, just debating, trying to learn, understand, synthesize. We could have taken it elsewhere, but the office is crowded and we couldn't find a quiet spot in the corner.

Never thought you were fighting, Tom. Let's go to the bar and I'll buy you a virtual.

TOM ~

Thanks, Robert. I'll take a gin and tonic. It is morning after all.

NAOMI ~

Why do you advise staying off the set, Alan? My background's in theatre production - I think it'd feel really weird not to be involved!

ALAN ~

There only a handful of possible outcomes, none good.

a) You dislike a performance or the director
b) You don't get paid
c) You fall in love with the director
d) Other writing stops, ABCDE becomes an obsession
e) The film is underfunded, no money for post
f) It's brilliant. Critics slam it. No TV deal.

Seriously, filmmaking is not theatre. You're not the 'playwright.' You have a superior talent for screenwriting, which I have congratulated several times, so take it as read. Go forth and write more. If you want to direct someday *DO NOT* understudy other film directors. Start by directing a short film of your own with a three-man crew.

NAOMI ~

Folks on another messageboard I use are assuring me this is a 'getting to know you' kind of meeting, where we'll probably just talk about the script and they can make sure I'm not some loony before it goes any further.

With that in mind, do you think it's a good idea to send them my CV (resume) beforehand, so they know a bit about me? It doesn't have any writing credits on it (they know that) but it'll tell them all about my creative background and management experience, and hopefully show them I've got my head screwed on. I thought about taking it to the meeting but then there'll be that awkward silence while they read it (or pretend to). Of course, I could just wait until they ask me, but then I'd have to remember all the pertinent details on the spot, and I'm hopeless when I'm put on the spot.

ALAN ~

ABSOLUTELY NOT!

The fact that you wrote ABCDE is all they (or I, or anyone else in show business) need to know. I have never presented a resume or been asked for one *as a writer*.

You're not applying for a job. Your task is to assess whether their offer is interesting. It probably won't be. Get ready to say no.

- Alan von Altendorf

NAOMI ~

Okay Alan, I hear ya! Thanks. :)

I need to present myself as an equal. I'm gonna find that hard as I'm so clueless. But everyone's gotta start somewhere I guess.

SALLY ~

Naomi, business negotiations are not unlike dating. If you come in feeling or looking desperate or needy, odds are you won't be happy with the outcome. If you come in with the understanding that you bring value to the table, you start off negotiating from a much more secure standpoint. People love to talk about themselves. Want to make a good impression? Let the other guy talk.

Negotiations are also like auditions in a way: they want to walk out of this with a new business relationship. They want everything to work. They want to like you. They want to say yes. It isn't adversarial. All you have to do is be your winning, charming, professional self, and they'll fall in love with you.

Listen. Ask questions. Take notes. Be engaged. Be genuinely interested. Be a human being and already that will set you apart.

RLB ~

You don't have to be humble to keep your mouth shut when dealing with people who have all the power. Keeping quiet and listening is being savvy.

JIM ~

I hope this turns out to be a real opportunity for you, Naomi.

BRIAN ~

Naomi, first, I don't think we've properly been introduced … nice to "meet" you. Second congrats on this meeting. I know it will be the first of many. My 2 cents:

You only have to be "professional" in your attitude. They are already interested in your script. No sales needed. These guys aren't agents or managers... if that were the case I would be ready with pitches and several scripts... but don't be surprised if these producers don't ask what else you are working on... I've been asked that at almost every meeting I've been in... it's an easy ice-breaker and if they like your writing style they will want to see your next script first... who wouldn't?

Ask them their plans for the film; distribution plans and especially what they plan the budget to be. Not only will it help you estimate their level of professionalism, but it will clue you in on their level of financing. If they say they are trying to raise money (which I'll bet they are) then be prepared to take a rain check for the time being, or a small down payment as an "option" agreement, but insist on a payday (in a contract) when Abcde GOES INTO PRODUCTION. Any points and a back-end deals for writers in the indy world is a one way trip to giving your work away. The exceptions are too few to mention. I would say that what ever you get up front is probably what you'll get paid.

Another question to ask is who wrote their last feature. Perhaps you could contact that writer and see how they fared. If the deal went well the producers would be happy to give you that info.

As far as being on set, I would ask for a visit perhaps when a particular scene is being shot. If you're not familiar with the process it could be detrimental to all involved. It may drive you and the director crazy... maybe not. You may have to witness the murder of your little darling. Test the water and see how it feels. Visit after the shoot has been going two or three days to let the crew and director get up speed (no pun intended.) Trust me on this. If it goes well you'll be back for more scenes.

There's a lot of great advice on this thread. You've got your foot in the door. It's a great step. Someone out there who has made a film likes your work! Yeah!

I look forward to following your journey. Best of luck and break a leg.

p.s. -

The WGA has salary information (including, I believe, fee ranges for indy productions) on their web site. I highly recommend you look those over. Knowledge is power, and you've got the power because you own the script they want.

Brian

NAOMI ~

Thanks Brian. Nice to meet you too :) Helpful advice.

========================= **four days later** =========================

NAOMI ~

Just thought I'd let you know the meeting was yesterday and went well - looks like I've fallen in with possibly the nicest people in the film industry! They're very excited about the script and very serious about getting production underway a.s.a.p. to be finished by this time next year. It sounds like they can get some good names attached and they're in with some decent distributors. All very exciting!

No contract's been signed yet but it'll happen over the next few days. They're offering me a percentage of the 'cash budget' - can anyone explain what that means, please?

BRIAN ~

I've never heard that term before but my guess is they are deferring payment to crew and getting in kind services etc. They have to raise a certain amount of cash to make the movie, so they are including the script in that budget amount, which could be pretty low.

For example if their movie budget is $500,000 but most of the crew is working on deferred (for free) and they are getting facilities, some equipment, locations donated, they have people working for points etc... then even though their budget is $500,000 they only have to raise $300,000.

Then they use state incentive money, rebates, maybe even some gap funding... the funds they need to raise are only $150,000... so, all they would need "cash" wise is $150,000 for a "$500,000" budget.

So, what they are saying to you is you get a percentage of the "cash" budget which at (let's pretend) 10% would be $15,000.

Now of course, none of my numbers mean anything, this is just a demonstration of what they COULD mean, but what I stated out above is how many a low budget film is financed.

They maybe really nice people, but don't give anything away.

NAOMI ~

Thank you, Brian.

Writing assignments

JULIE ANN ~

Hey, Barry. How did you manage to get script writing assignments before you wrote a spec? Are you a professional writer in another arena?

BARRY C. ~

I'm sorry if I wasn't clear. I wrote the spec first, and then used it as a writing sample to get assignments. I got my first commission from having my script on Inktip. For tax reasons, Canadian productions really want Canadian writers -- and in a country with a total population of only 32 million (pretty darn small for the second largest country in the world) you have a lot less competition.

So, lucky small fish in a small pond. :-)

Then once you have a produced credit, it gets a lot easier to get people to talk to you.

The way it's been working for me, is that the producer will have an idea for the film he wants to make. My first was a sequel, so he gave me the script from the first one and told me he wanted to introduce one more main character, told me he had Roddy Piper (Canadian wrestling star turned actor) coming back for the second film -- but could only afford him for three days shooting, so his part must fit into that shooting schedule, but he still wanted the character to appear throughout the film. We discussed his effects budget and certain things he wanted in the film (he wanted the boy lead to fly, he wanted a wolf creature somewhere in there, etc). We also discussed things like what locations he had access to. So I came up with my own storyline that could fill his wish list and wrote a treatment which he submitted to his executive producer. The exec released the development funds based on the treatment. The producer wrote up a contract for me and upon receipt of the first payment I got started on the script.

All my commissions have followed a similar pattern. I discuss the producer's wants, wishes, and requirements (sometimes they have an idea what they want the story to be about, sometimes it's open or vague like: "I want to do a disaster film, what can you come up with? – and oh yeah, I want something blowing up in a tunnel or cave! The fireball will look cool." (I swear, that's what he said!)

I come up with a storyline and write the treatment. The development funds get released based on that treatment or pitch. I start writing the script upon first payment.

As for payment, I receive 50% up front and 50% on first day of principal photography. I negotiate my fee based on the project's budget.

I'm lucky enough to have such a good working relationship with the producer I do most of my work for, that on more than one occasion he's sent me contracts paying more than my quote because the exec upped the original budget based on the treatment! :-)

ROB ~

There are a few pros (Brian, Jim, Alan, Naomi for instance) and you, who've given some very insightful info to the office here. I for one have learned a lot from these posts.

I'd love to read at least some of that spec you wrote. I've read some of Brian's and Naomi's work. I'd love to see some of Jim's too. The reason of my interest is purely education. So many books and/or good intentioned writers tell how the script is suppose to look like, but I'd like to see one's that's sold.

I used to write and be in the biz a very long time ago, when tech [camera direction and "scene" terms] could be included. Lately I've been refraining from putting any in. Do you think that'd give a producer the impression the writer can't write a script that could be used to shoot from?

BARRY C. ~

I'm afraid I don't know the answers to all you questions, but I'll chime in on what I do know.

For the producer I do most of my work for, the "exec" is the investor. That's where the some of the basic requirements come from, such as budget -- simply how much money he's willing to invest in a film this time round (yes, they come back looking to make another as soon as they see profit from the first one!) They may have an idea that they want a film in a certain genre or have an idea like "Ghostbusters but with kids" which was the order for GHOST TRAP currently in post production. As for how much the development funds are, I don't know but I'm sure it includes some upfront $ for the producer and anyone else he wants to contract in the early stages. With this producer, I don't have to worry about "if" it goes to production, just when.

Another producer I work for does it differently, he gets the development money from someone, pays my upfront for the script, and when its finished, goes looking for the rest of the money from investors and Film Board Funds. This guy is looking for much higher $ as his project is intended for the big screen.

Third producer, I'm just getting to know his operation better, so I don't know where his money comes from, but he produces 7 to 9 Movie of the Week each year. I'm hoping we become very good friends :-)

Inktip / logline advice?

DAVE ~

I've had "Who Iced Frosty?" on Inktip for a few months now. Gotten tons of logline "views" or "reads", but only one download of the script/synopsis. Inktip says that if this happens, then your logline probably needs work. But then, maybe that's Inktip promising too much to its clients? I know people who never got a single download of their script on Inktip in six months.

Inktip says the logline is supposed to be under 60 words. I tried to make mine as succinct as possible, but the story's a bit left-field: fanciful comedy film noir spoof. Perhaps that doesn't get across. I know the story's not for every producer, yadda yadda, but if I can write a better logline, I'll do it.

Opinions? Does this suck?

"A private eye and his sidekick investigate the murder of Frosty the Snowman on Christmas Eve and find themselves embroiled in the shady underworld of the Easter Bunny, Santa Claus and Tooth Fairy, while dodging a gang of snowmen hell-bent on avenging their leader."

ALAN ~

The problem is that it's L7 (square, no edge, rated G for kiddies)

Try this: "Carmelli's the name, like it says on the door. I used to be a cop. Still have the badge. Comes in handy when I have to get tough with the dames. Especially on Christmas Eve, when somebody put his hand in the wrong pocket and wound up dead in a big sloppy puddle. Noir satire."

DAVE ~

Maybe I'll try a complete rethink. Would still like to include some story elements. I've posted the radio script in the Files section.

ROB ~

Dave, did you see the message line below about the one sentence?

You may have done a superb job with the craft on your script but it could be no one likes the story, who the "F" knows.

JIM ~

Why do the PI and his sidekick have to dodge the gang of snowmen? From the logline, it seems they would be allies since they're both looking for whoever killed Frosty.

DAVE ~

That's the thing. I wanted to make it one sentence without so much detail. The detective and partner follow the trail from suspect to suspect, just as the snowmen are closing in, so they (the snowmen) assume the duo are either complicit or else have information they want. Can't say all that in a logline, though, but I wanted to highlight some additional danger/antagonism.

And Rob, you're entirely right... maybe at face value, the story sounds like crap. But this script is meant as farce. How does a logline get that across? Farcical comedy loglines seem especially hard.

Airplane! -- A veteran fighter pilot must overcome his past trauma in order to land a passenger jet after the crew falls ill from food poisoning.

Monte Python's Holy Grail: King Arthur recruits a group of knights for a quest to find the Holy Grail.

Stunningly boring compared to what the final movies were like.

But I'm okay with it. Just wondered if there's a solution I haven't thought of. And shout-outs to the B-Listers. I wanted to put the question to this group first, for good reason.

Kudos, hats off and backslaps,

Dave

ALAN ~

Dave sez he posted FROSTY (radio drama) in the Files.

Recommended **F** for funny and **P** as in please read it, to give Dave some feedback before we roll to record.

Thanks.

A query letter for Aquarianna

BRIAN ~

I composed a query letter for my graphic novel "Aquarianna." I have targeted a few agents looking for exactly the type of project that this is but want to make sure they check out the website. Any thoughts, comments, or critiques would be greatly appreciated.

Dear _____,

I am seeking representation for my latest project, "Aquarianna," a graphic novel that utilizes the talents of Iain McCaig, the world-renowned concept artist behind Star Wars I, II, III, Harry Potter, and The Terminator. Along with Iain's designs comes the artistic talents of Liberum Donum, the illustrators behind "Kingdoms of Grace."

Aquarianna is a historical adventure fantasy set in the mid-1800's; when mermaids and monsters still existed and sailing ships ruled the seas.

To stop a horrific sea serpent and its monstrous master, a young sailor must steal a mermaid from a ruthless freak-show owner only to discover that she is the girl he loved... who drowned three years before.

I have posted a finished, five-page prologue on the Aquarianna web site along with several concept and character designs for your review.

www.aquarianna.com

The script is available upon request. I look forward to hearing from you.

Respectfully,
Brian Young

ALAN ~

Dear _____,

I'm seeking representation for "Aquarianna," a graphic novel that utilizes the artistic talents of Iain McCaig and Liberum Donum.

McCaig is the world-renowned concept artist behind Star Wars I, II, III, Harry Potter, and The Terminator. Donum is the famed illustrator who created "Kingdoms of Grace."

A five-page story synopsis is available at www.aquarianna.com with extensive concept and character designs for your review.

Aquarianna is an adventure fantasy set in the 1800's when mermaids and monsters still existed and sailing ships ruled the seas.

To stop a horrific sea serpent and its monstrous master, a young sailor must steal a mermaid from a ruthless London freak-show owner, only to discover that she is the girl he loved ... and who drowned three years before.

The graphic novel script (and feature film screenplay) is available on request. I look forward to hearing from you.

Respectfully,
Brian Young

JIM ~

Are your seeking representation for the graphic novel or a screenplay based upon same? It's unclear.

The logline definitely needs work. To stop them from doing what? The word "must" scrambles the verb tense. Too many unnecessary adjectives? Generally awkward. I get the story, but a smooth logline for this one is a bit of a challenge. I don't think you can pull it off in one sentence.

Maybe...

A young sailor's plan to stop a marauding sea serpent requires the services of a mermaid, so he steals (kidnaps?) one from a traveling freak show. He gets the surprise of his life when he discovers his new ally is actually his lost love, missing since a boating accident three years earlier.

BRIAN ~

Thanks Jim, I 'll work on that logline.

JIM ~

Just checked out your website. Wow!

Did you have to invest a lot of $$$ to get it looking that good?

ALAN ~

Terrif, ain't it? A+ … and graphic novel nails story copyright.

BRIAN ~

Just between us B-listers I got a "cease and desist" letter about my title from an attorney last week. What a pain. I had to lawyer-up. My guy is a trademark/copyright bulldog and he shut the whole legal attack down, but it still cost me way too much.

Deal or No Deal ?

DAVE ~

Howdy all! Some interesting news came up:

My writing partner and I got an offer from a producer on Inktip to buy our low-budget script. Would be a first sale for us both.

He says the university he teaches film at can put up $20K in funding, so he's offered $500 up front and $500 on completion of production, and 5% of net producer's revenue. Wants to start shooting in 4 weeks. (I imagine it might be a student production type thing?) He says he's landed worldwide distro on his past films.

My partner was looking into filming it himself and he was in talks with funding agencies and venues, though he never made a film before. We're wondering whether to take the deal or go this route instead, travel the steeper hill, and keep all rights, etc.

I'm not so concerned about the money, but more about getting credit, and having a final product I'd be proud to put on my resume, which would hopefully lead to bigger and better things. We initially wrote this script just to write something sellable. I don't consider it my chef-d'oeuvre.

Should I care or just take the deal, cross fingers, and move on? No big expectations about that back-end money, but anyone care to comment on such a deal? What would you do?

ALAN ~

As you know, I like to put trip wires and fences around various promises. Must show university funding is approved for your script. Must show production budget and principal cast. Must start shooting within 60 days. Five points of producer's net is by definition zero. You want two points of world gross. Audited.

What has this guy successfully produced and directed before? Ask him to send you a DVD. Make sure his name is on screen credits as producer/director.

I'm tempted to outbid him.

JIM ~

I wouldn't look at this as a money deal, because it's not. There will be no net profits.

I suggest you approach it as a way to get a feature writing credit in your resume. If he can convince you it will for sure get made, make the deal.

> *"Five points of producer's net is by definition zero."*

It would be fun to make up a little dictionary of what motion picture industry terms really mean.

ALAN ~

Casting ... advertising a project to raise money
Warm personal regards ... no further contact desired
Negative Pickup ... no deal if they decide they don't like the movie
Completion bond ... 12% cash penalty to get Negative Pickup
Agent (1) ... unavailable rude person who says "no"
Agent (2) ... story thief who says "yes" and charges fees
Producer ... casino player with Other People's Money
Director ... unreasonable sadist
Choreographer ... unreasonable masochist

DAVE ~

Thanks for chiming in, Alan and Jim! Helps to get some perspective.

Alan, by "Must show production budget and principal cast" do you mean before we agree, or later on once he's established these things, as part of the agreement?

Clearly we don't see it as a big-money deal, and thanks to reads on the B-List and other sources, I'm aware that "back-end" usually translates in to no-end. Getting credit on a feature is important though, and since it's going cheap for a cheap production, we're going to try to keep as many rights as we can. Thinking of asking for:

- $500 up front then the balance of 5% of final budget (since he said he's looking for more funding, and it looks like his previous films have hovered around $100K in budget.)

- world-wide theatre rights (this is a one-location that could be adapted for stage, which is why we'd ask)

- he gets up to 2 more drafts, then the script is locked

- sole writing credit

- sequel rights

- 2 percent of gross

Reasonable?
Unheard of?
"You'll never work in this town again"?

ALAN ~

As a general rule, ask for more. Negotiation always involves compromise. Be prepared to "take away the sale" if you can't get the deal you want. Tell us about the project. Is it the two guys in the cubicles?

LUCY ~

2% of the gross is a starting point, and actually a high one. Don't be surprised if it ends with something like 0.085% of the gross which is an average. Also, because it is so low budget and through a university, it is likely there will be no offer at all on the gross; that the producer's offer off his net was just to make the deal appear sweeter to you.

DAVE ~

It's a killer-thriller set in a barn. Done strictly for a quick indie sale, to get a foot in the door. Approached it like a writing assignment: had fun with it, but not the kind of thing I'd normally write or watch myself. It was a top 3 on Zoe a few months ago.

We're going to send our reply today, so if anyone has more thoughts on our "list of demands" above (thanks, Lucy), let no opinions be barred! I'll keep you all posted and send as many details as permitted.

ALAN ~

Oh. That's entirely different. Sell it. Screenplay by Alan Smithee.

BARRY C. ~

Way to Go, David!

As long as you wrote it for just such an occasion, and the occasion looks legitimate... go for it.

What caught my eye though, is the 2 more drafts. Just make sure you're willing to do two major re-writes (worst case scenario) for your share of the $1000 (and if he wants to start shooting in 4 weeks he's going to want those pages fast!) BTW, have you had any discussion at all about what kind of changes he'd be looking for? Believe me, nothing is worse than being contractually obligated to destroy a perfectly good script... it sucks the life right out of you. :-(

I'd personally prefer the second $500 on first day of principle photography before it get's spent somewhere else :-) So take a deep breath... make sure you're alright with it all, and if you are, take some of the money and go celebrate Brother! Congratulations on your first sale!

DAVE ~

Thanks, Barry! And more thanks due to Alan for providing a private haven to discuss this. I'd never post it on the main boards!

We haven't accepted yet. Sent in a counter offer. Will keep you all posted.

ALAN ~

Spelling police: principal photography

DAVE ~

Principal Photography used to call me in his office after class because he wanted to take some rather unprincipled photographs...

So we sent in "a list of our demands" (pretty much what I posted above, though a little more $ up front). Got a reply a few hours later saying "I know we can reach an agreement from here. We are not too far apart" and that he'd send a full response tomorrow.

So we're optimistic.

================= **the following day** =================

DAVE ~

He counter-offered 2% of the final budget, and we eventually settled on 3.5% (with a minimum we're happy with), so he met us halfway.

And agreed to all other terms. Goes to show that if you don't ask, you don't get. Waiting for the contracts now.

Thanks to everyone for advice!

RLB ~

Sounds like a good strategy to me. Congratulations and best of success with this venture!

DAVE ~

Thanks, RLB. But there's always a snag! The department head at the producer's university wants to read the script this weekend.

This is a Catholic university, and he said they don't want to fund something that will 'come back to haunt them' (nice choice of phrase!) The producer seems to think this won't be a problem, but you never know. I told him don't worry, we were both raised Catholic and I own my own church. Plus my aunt's a Dominican nun (retired) in Belgium and knows the lyrics to "Dominique" in French and Flemish.

The script actually explores a bunch of moral issues and isn't just a plain horror/slasher story, so we might be okay. Also there's no scene where a coked-up Pope crashes his Popemobile into a group of schoolchildren, so we should be alright.

================== **four days later** =-================

DAVE ~

No deal.

Got a msg from the producer this morning and the university department head "found the contents unacceptable for a student project."
Thanks, religion!

Oh well, back to the ol' drawing board.

RLB ~

Too bad. At least you know the reason. I had someone tell me once,
he loved my story, but there were "problems" with it, and he said he
would email me details. He never did.

ALAN ~

The good news is that the producer went to bat for you. There is no
way to "process" this kind of disappointment. All I can say is that
Columbia had a 7-person committee in the 1990s. My project cleared
a reader and a development v.p. who took it to the committee.

I lost 3-4. One effing vote out of seven.

Zombies vs Gladiators

JIM ~

Roy Price, who heads up Amazon's attempt to launch a movie studio, found a script he liked called ZOMBIE vs GLADIATORS.

The original script needed a lot of work, so Roy set up a rewrite competition. The idea was that anyone could try their hand at a rewrite, and the writer, who in Amazon's opinion does the best job, wins $10,000.

I hadn't planned on entering, but then over the weekend, I got an idea for fixing the script, so I gave it a shot.

Posted about it on the main board, and now all the artistes are going to brand me a hack. LOL! The competition ended yesterday with some 67 rewrite drafts entered. Mine is [posted to Zoetrope].

ALAN ~

Kalergis does rewrite in a couple days, just like the Golden Age.

ROB ~

Hack!

Does yer wife bitch for wearing your fedora in the house?

:-}

Hope you win.

JIM ~

[grin] Fastest rewrite in the West, pardner! Seriously, speed counts for a lot in my niche. Folks want stuff yesterday.

Amazon gave notes on the original, and they were pretty specific, also very smart. I found out that the head of the operation wrote those notes, so I approached the task as if I was working for any client... doing my best to help them realize their vision.

Looking over the competition it became evident that only a few had any clue what it meant to take notes or how to implement them. Many wrote page 1 rewrites based upon their own vision... fatal mistake.

I figured it would be between me and two or three others as to who would take home the check. I also figured it might be a way for me to pick up Roy Price, the studio head, as a client. Normally I wouldn't work on somebody elses script on spec, but hey, I could use an extra $10k about now.

[to Rob] ~ She's ok with the fedora, but she does give me some crap on my beret days.

ALAN ~

Important thread, folks. Show business for real.

BILL ~

Didn't read the original, or know the content of the notes, but read your rewrite, Jim. Whilst I hate horror movies, I thoroughly enjoyed your version and think that you must be in with a good chance of winning that $10K. It's a highly entertaining story which I enjoyed immensely.

JIM ~

Thanks! I had fun writing it. Cracked myself up a couple of times.

If you've got some time on your hands, you might find it interesting to see how I incorporated the studio notes in my rewrite draft.

BILL ~

Thanks for making those available, Jim. I'll download them and compare to your rewrite as I'm sure that there's lots I can learn from the exercise.

[later] ~ Thank you for providing such a useful educational experience. When you ever get around to writing that book on screen-writing, please make sure that you include this material as it teaches a lesson that as far as I know is unavailable elsewhere, i.e., how to go about rewriting a script (in its own right) and how to address studio notes and give effect to them. What makes this lesson all the more valuable is the fact that the original script was itself decent, but your rewrite definitely improved it, and more importantly gave effect to the studio notes.

I might sound like a sycophant for saying this, Jim, but I am not. This is my sincere opinion. What you did and the material you kindly made available here to tyros like me is indispensable and a real tour de force. Thank you.

After reading the notes and your rewrite, I also think that you must be the odds-on favourite to win that $10K.

All the best, mate.

    Bill.

JIM ~

You're welcome, Bill, and thanks for the kind words. When I'm rich and famous, you can be my publicist!

One of the things I like about Alan's office is that I can put up stuff like this, and it's usually met with intelligence and sanity. When I post anything more advanced than How Many Brads on the main board, for the most part, I get back a whooshing sound as the words fly over heads.

Contributors

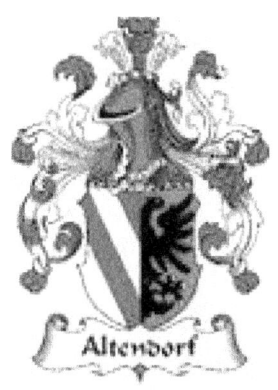

ALAN VON ALTENDORF

I've had a busy life. Three 16mm shorts, six screenplays, three novels, two nonfiction books, three feature film credits, prime time episodic, network news, local TV, corporate videos, radio comedy, celebrity chat, opera, Lake Tahoe shows, music videos, advertising, technical writing, business management, and graphic arts. On weekends, I was a pirate.

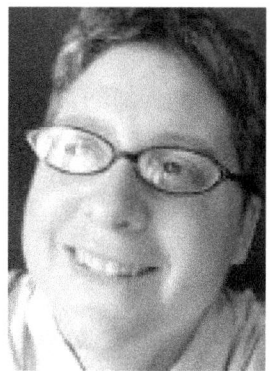

HEATHER MCLOUD

Heather writes novels and short stories based on Steven King's dictum to write a certain number of 'bad words' each day. She explores diverse issues spanning the range of human experience -- crises of faith, encounters with the supernatural, and loss of loved ones. Her best work is produced at coffee shops or in the company of a sleeping dog, which she lets lie.

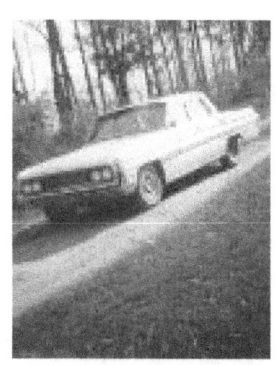

RLB HARTMANN

The Olds is LuciBuck's first car, which she frequently drove at 70 mph on a lonely country two-lane to teach English in the next county over. At that time, she was writing a western novel which remains incognito despite interest in the script version by a well-known actor. She has dabbled in poetry, short stories, essays, and irate letters to the editor. Planning to write a 600-page spoof of every Western ever shown, she instead became inspired to complete *Tierra del Oro*, a 9-book series of historical novels (The Cordero Saga). www.rlbhartmann.com

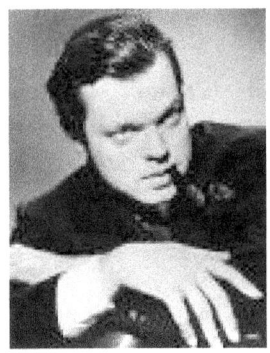

JIM KALERGIS

Jim is a Hollywood story analyst, rewrite specialist, and educator. Expanded versions of many of his B-List posts will be a part of forthcoming books "Magic Screenwriting" and "Screen Story Analysis."

See www.screenplayrewrite.com

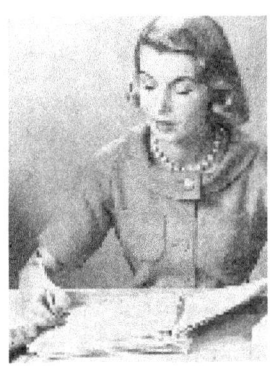

SALLY LEWIS

Sally Lewis is the pseudonym of a writer, ghostwriter and editor.

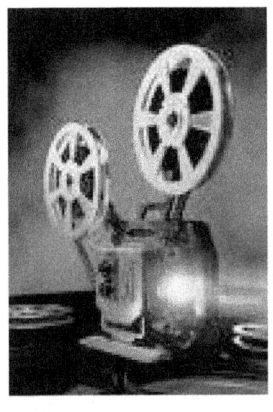

JOHN CORRAL

After a long and successful career as a mime, John Corral is now trying to speak through his writing. At first it was all blank space, true to John's earlier calling, but more recently he's managed to yield the words "Mama" and "Papa" as recognizable scrawls from his writing instrument of choice: a quill and ink. He hopes to make the transition to fountain pen soon. A relentless overachiever, John tried to cook grits in the same amount of time that the witness in My Cousin Vinny said it took him: 5 minutes.

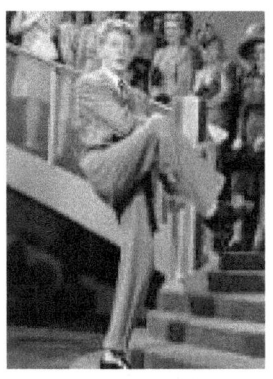

BILL SHERWOOD

Bill Sherwood is a dilettante. He has the academic credentials to prove that he knows a great deal about not very much. He retired from professional life over 30 years ago to devote himself to hedonism and philanthropy, not necessarily in that order.

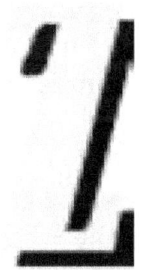

BARRY S. COWAN

After too many years of endless hours and devotion as a noted private investigator and bodyguard, Barry gave up "the life" to find a personal life of his own. He landed in the advertising industry and this too became an 80 hour a week position. Barry now writes and lives happily ever after with his beautiful wife and two terrific kids which he gets to hug and kiss every day.

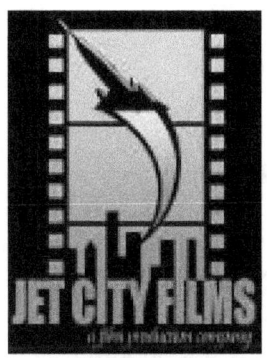

BRIAN A. YOUNG

I am a writer, director and producer of independent films, mostly narrative features with a few shorts or a documentary thrown in for good measure.

My work has been produced, optioned, won awards, and shown on the big screen. I have been honored to helm other people's projects and lucky enough to have worked with some incredibly talented, ultra-creative individuals. Filmmaking is a group effort.

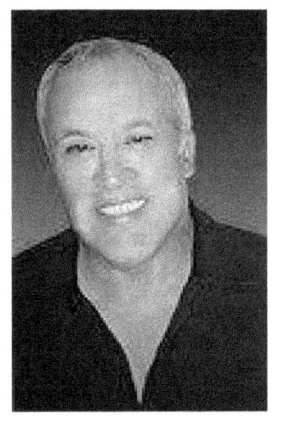

TONY CONTRERAS

Tony says he is an unpublished author who couldn't get elected dog catcher and spends most days looking for his swing on the golf course: "Like Satchel Paige, I don't like to look back, someone may be gaining on me."

EASTSIDE starring Mario Lopez was based on the story of Tony's life. He is an award-winning Amazon Studios semifinalist, Best Dialogue Track, for his original script and feature length storyboard of 'Xochitl' (2010). Screenplays: 'Amigos' (2010) 'Xtreme Flyers' (2011). Working on *Granpa is a Trip* for the Amazon Studios 2012 TV contest.

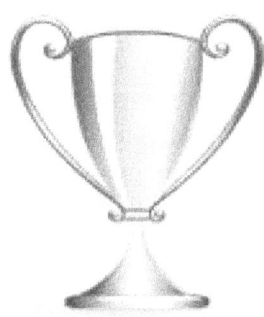

ERIK SVEHAUG

B-List Silver Cup for Fiction: "Drum School"

Erik's work has appeared in Ampersand, Bartleby-Snopes, Linnet's, Metazen, Static Movement, BinnaclesUltraShort, Bannock Street Books' Outlaws, Dead Mule School, Qarrtsiluni, Tales of Old, and Hall Bros.

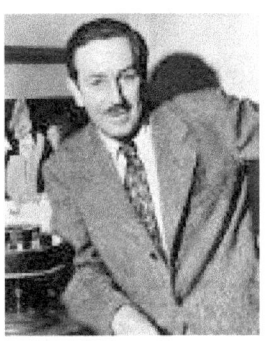

ROB WILLIAMSON

Rob is a founding member of the B-List, with over 2000 posts. In addition to contributing anecdotes from the set of ANIMAL HOUSE, THE BLUES BROTHERS and numerous other adventures, we owe Rob special thanks for making this book possible by telephoning Alan and pouring on five tons of charm.

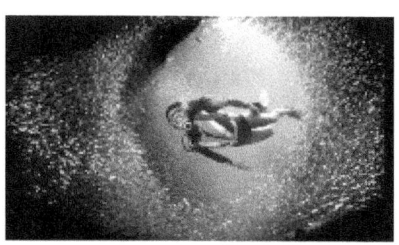

LUCY SOGOIAN

When not riding the waves or playing under the sea, Lucy gets paid to make bad writing good and good writing great.

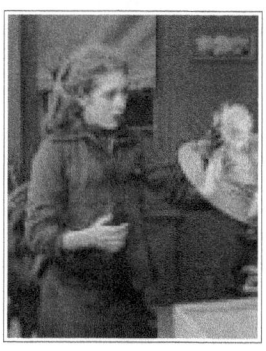

NAOMI JAMES

Naomi has spent her career so far helping other people tell their stories, but really longs to tell her own. She signed her first screenplay option agreement during the writing of this book and hopes to sign many more.

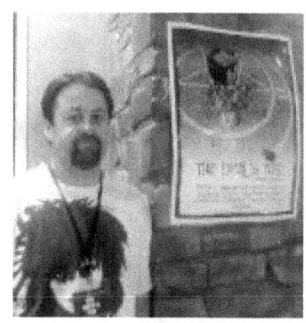

CHRIS KEATON

While inside escaping Arizona heat Chris decided to listen to those voices in his head and write. With a lot of screenplays written and a book on the way his hobby has become an addiction.

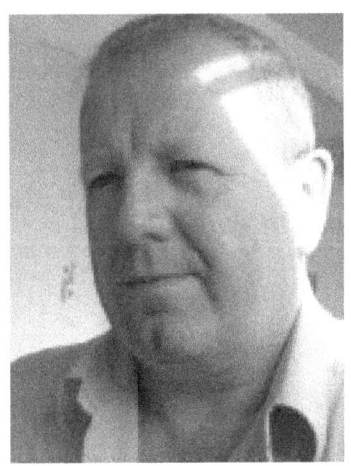

GERRY BYRON

I started selling short stories in my twenties. Recently selected for a BBC comedy writers team, but left when I realised the producer was certifiably insane. I've made two short films and written several features, one of which made the Nichol QF. I'm British, Scottish, happily agnostic. My sense of humour is like my coffee - black, with no sugar please.

Subject
Index

Dialogue

Directors

Films

Film Production

Loglines

Scenes

Scene Cards

Screenplays

Screenwriters

Screenwriting

<u>Writing</u>

www.ingramcontent.com/pod-product-compliance
Lightning Source LLC
Chambersburg PA
CBHW051451170526
45166CB00001B/202